DK EYEWITNESS

T0047000

TOP 10 STOCKHOLM

Top 10 Stockholm Highlights

Welcome to Stockholm **5**
Exploring Stockholm **6**
Stockholm Highlights **10**
Skansen **12**
Vasamuseet **14**
Stockholm Archipelago **16**
Stadshuset **22**
Drottningholm **24**
The Royal Palace (Kungliga Slottet) **26**
Gröna Lund **28**
Nordiska Museet **30**
Historiska Museet **32**
Hagaparken **34**

The Top 10 of Everything

Moments in History **38**
Churches **40**
Museums and Galleries **42**
Parks and Gardens **44**
Off the Beaten Path **46**
Children's Attractions **48**
Pubs and Bars **50**
Cafés **52**
Restaurants **54**
Places to Shop for Swedish Design **56**
Stockholm for Free **58**
Festivals and Events **60**

CONTENTS

Stockholm Area by Area

Norrmalm and City **64**
Kungsholmen and Vasastan **70**
Östermalm and Djurgården **76**
Gamla Stan, Skeppsholmen and Blasieholmen **84**
Södermalm **92**
Further Afield **98**

Streetsmart

Getting Around **106**
Practical Information **108**
Places to Stay **112**

General Index **118**
Acknowledgments **124**
Phrase Book **126**

Within each Top 10 list in this book, no hierarchy of quality or popularity is implied. All 10 are, in the editor's opinion, of roughly equal merit.

Title page, front cover and spine *The serene Gamla Stan waterfront at dusk*
Back cover, clockwise from top left *Floor-to-ceiling bookcases, Stadsbibliotek; Archipelago covered in snow; Stockholm's cityscape; Gamla Stan; Södermalm waterfront*

The rapid rate at which the world is changing is constantly keeping the DK Eyewitness team on our toes. While we've worked hard to ensure that this edition of Stockholm is accurate and up-to-date, we know that opening hours alter, standards shift, prices fluctuate, places close and new ones pop up in their stead. So, if you notice we've got something wrong or left something out, we want to hear about it. Please get in touch at **travelguides@dk.com**

Welcome to Stockholm

Grand royal palaces and lush green parks. Densely packed Old Town streets and a sprawling archipelago. Swimming in peaceful Lake Mälaren by day and checking out the buzzing restaurant and bar scene in Södermalm by night. The Swedish capital is a city of amazing contrasts, and with DK Eyewitness Top 10 Stockholm, it's yours to explore.

The biggest city in Scandinavia, Stockholm is your gateway to a world of clean and compact living, sleek design and rustic cuisine. It is a place of short crisp winter days and long balmy summer nights. The city is made up of numerous islands, many with their own distinctive character, from colourful and historic **Gamla Stan** to leafy **Djurgården** and elegant **Östermalm**.

Witness the vestiges of the ill-fated 17th-century warship *Vasa* at the incredible **Vasamuseet**, before delving deeper into the country's history at **Nordiska Museet** and **Historiska Museet**. Behold the pomp and splendour of the Swedish monarchy at **Drottningholm** and the **Royal Palace (Kungliga Slottet)**. Take in sweeping panoramic views from the tall tower of **Stadshuset**, get away from it all at **Hagaparken** or **Skansen**, or ride a seafront roller coaster at **Gröna Lund** theme park. Or simply share in the typically Swedish coffee-and-cake ritual *fika*, and watch the world go by through the window of a trendy café.

Whether you're visiting for a weekend or a week, our Top 10 guide brings together the best of everything the city can offer, from hip **Södermalm** to sophisticated **Kungsholmen**. The guide has useful tips throughout, from seeking out what's free to getting off the beaten path, plus eight easy-to-follow itineraries, designed to tie together a clutch of sights in a short space of time. Add inspiring photography and detailed maps, and you have the essential pocket-sized travel companion. **Enjoy the book, and enjoy Stockholm.**

Clockwise from top: **Nybroviken harbour, Gamla Stan, Stadsbiblioteket, Vaxholm Island, Stockholm Archipelago, Ericsson Globe, frozen Riddarfjärden, Brantingtorget at Gamla Stan**

Exploring Stockholm

With so many islands, activities and attractions to experience, it can be hard to know where to begin when it comes to discovering this surprising city. These two sightseeing itineraries will help you get the very best out of your visit to Stockholm.

The Nordiska Museet offers a comprehensive look at Swedish cultural history.

Two Days in Stockholm

Day ❶

MORNING

Start at the excellent **Vasamuseet** *(see pp14–15)* before taking a stroll through Galärparken to the **Nordiska Museet** *(see pp30–31)*. **Ulla Winbladh** *(see p81)* is nearby for a traditional Swedish lunch.

AFTERNOON

Take the tram along **Strandvägen** *(see p79)* towards Strömkajen and take a ferry to the **Stockholm Archipelago** *(see pp16–17)*. Pack a picnic and make the short trip to Fjäderholmarna, where you can swim from the rocks.

Day ❷

MORNING

Arrive early at **Stadshuset** *(see pp22–3)* to admire panoramic views from its tower. Tour **Kungliga Slottet** or the **Royal Palace** *(see pp26–7)* then wander the narrow streets of **Gamla Stan** *(see pp84–91)* with its many shops, cafés and restaurants.

AFTERNOON

Take the ferry from Slussen across to **Djurgården** *(see p45)*, before taking a stroll around **Skansen** *(see pp12–13)*. Then make for **Gröna Lund** amusement park *(see pp28–9)*, and end the day at the quirky ABBA-themed musical dining experience at *Mamma Mia! The Party* (booking is essential).

Four Days in Stockholm

Day ❶

MORNING

Hire City Bikes *(available Apr–Oct; citybikes.se)* and pedal around **Hagaparken** *(see pp34–5)*. From there it is not far to **Kungsholmen** *(see pp70–74)* island, where **Petite France** *(see p74)* is a decent place to have lunch.

The *Vasa* is the star of the Vasamuseet.

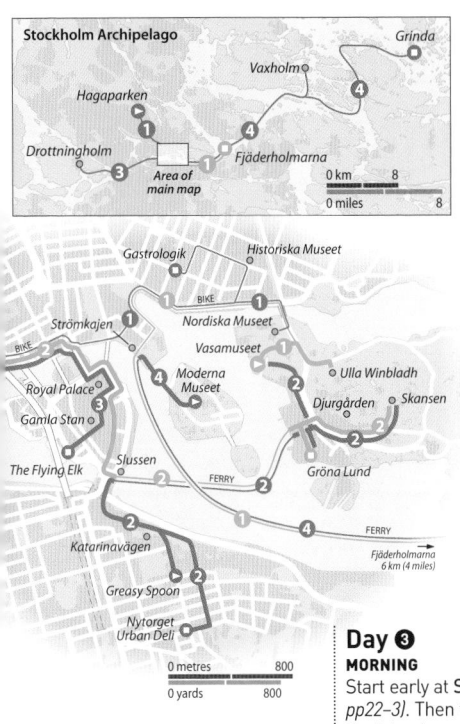

The island of Gamla Stan is the historic centre of Stockholm.

AFTERNOON
Cycle along the waterfront to the **Historiska Museet** *(see pp32–3)* and the **Nordiska Museet** *(see pp30–31)*. Then treat yourself to a high-end dinner at **Ekstedt** or **Gastrologik** *(see p81)*.

Day ❷

MORNING
Start with breakfast at **Greasy Spoon** *(see p96)*, before taking in the views from Katarinavägen on your walk down to Slussen. From there hop on a shuttle boat across to **Djurgården** *(see p45)* and check out the fascinating **Vasamuseet** *(see pp14–15)*.

AFTERNOON
Explore **Skansen** *(see pp12–13)* or **Gröna Lund** *(see pp28–9)*. Hop back on the boat and return to Slussen, before experiencing the nightlife of hip **Södermalm** *(see pp92–7)* after dinner at **Nytorget Urban Deli** *(see p97)*.

Day ❸

MORNING
Start early at **Stadshuset** *(see pp22–3)*. Then take a boat at Stadshusbron for a cruise along Lake Mälaren to the Royal Palace, **Drottningholm** *(see pp24–5)*.

AFTERNOON
Visit the **Royal Palace (Kungliga Slottet)** *(see pp26–7)* and the **Livrustkammaren** *(see p59)* armoury in the vaults beneath. Explore quaint **Gamla Stan** *(see pp84–91)*, before dining at **The Flying Elk** *(see p91)*.

Day ❹

MORNING
Begin the day at **Moderna Museet** *(see p86)*. If it is the weekend, you can enjoy brunch at the café's buffet *(see p90)*.

AFTERNOON
Set sail from nearby Strömkajen to the **Stockholm Archipelago** *(see pp16–17)*. Fjäderholmarna is 20 minutes away and perfect for picnics and swimming. If you wish to extend your journey, head to historic Vaxholm or pretty Grinda and stay another night.

Top 10 Stockholm Highlights

Yachts moored among the islets of the Stockholm Archipelago

Stockholm Highlights **10**

Skansen **12**

Vasamuseet **14**

Stockholm Archipelago **16**

Stadshuset **22**

Drottningholm **24**

The Royal Palace (Kungliga Slottet) **26**

Gröna Lund **28**

Nordiska Museet **30**

Historiska Museet **32**

Hagaparken **34**

TOP 10 Stockholm Highlights

A city of contrasts dictated by the weather, Stockholm can offer Christmas-card scenes in winter and sun-drenched quaysides and waterways in summer. Unique museums and cool nightlife make it a year-round destination, but do wrap up in the winter.

1 Skansen

Part re-creation of Swedish traditional life and part children's fair, this hilly park has something for everyone *(see pp12–13)*.

2 Vasamuseet

Get up close to the Vasa, which sank in Stockholm harbour on its maiden voyage in 1628 *(see pp14–15)*.

3 Stockholm Archipelago

An entire summer would not be enough to explore the archipelago's beaches, forests and seaside restaurants *(see pp16–17)*.

4 Stadshuset

The City Hall belies its stark exterior with magnificent halls, including the Prince's Gallery. The tower offers stunning views *(see pp22–3)*.

5 Drottningholm

Home to the royal family, this UNESCO World Heritage Site takes visitors back to 17th- and 18th-century grandeur. The extensive gardens are a delight *(see pp24–5)*.

6 The Royal Palace (Kungliga Slottet)

Built 57 years after its predecessor burned down in 1697, the Royal Palace is an extravagant combination of Italian, French and Swedish architectural influences *(see pp26–7)*.

7 Gröna Lund

Merging the best traditions of fairgrounds with thrill rides, Gröna Lund has something for everyone, from the 19th-century carousel to free-fall towers *(see pp28–9)*.

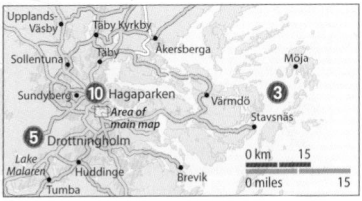

0 metres 500
0 yards 500

Nordiska Museet 8

Experience the Swedish way of life from the 16th to the 21st centuries in this museum, home to over 1.5 million exhibits – from jewellery to Strindberg's paintings *(see pp30–31)*.

9 Historiska Museet

Opened in 1943, this museum made its name with exhibits from the Viking era, as well as its collections from the early Middle Ages *(see pp32–3)*.

Hagaparken 10

A green oasis on the city's northern edge, this English-style park reveals its secrets along winding paths *(see pp34–5)*.

Top 10 Skansen

This open-air museum, which visualises Swedish history through the ages, was founded in 1891. It contains over 150 traditional buildings from around the country, dating from the 14th to the early 20th century – dismantled, transported and rebuilt on site. Nordic animals are kept in their natural habitats, surrounded by trees and plants from all over Sweden. Skansen changes naturally with the seasons – it's lively in summer, and calm and serene in winter.

1 Bredablick Tower

This 30-m- (98-ft-) high brick tower, was built by a royal physician who thought the views would be beneficial to people's wellbeing. It is no longer open to the public. Kids will enjoy the electric cars near the tower.

2 Funicular Railway

The mountain railway, Skansen's Bergbana, was built in 1897. Cable operated, it starts at the Hazelius entrance and is perfect for visitors with buggies or wheelchairs, or those simply wanting to enjoy a ride.

3 Historical Buildings

In the 19th-century town quarter, staff in traditional attire bake bread or make pottery. There are many farmsteads, churches and halls; several are open to the public.

4 Solliden Stage

Built in 1938, Skansen's iconic shell-shaped event space hosts gigs and concerts. Many famous artists have performed here.

5 Galejan Fairground

Enjoy the hand-painted carousels **(left)** and traditional sideshows.

Främmestad Windmill, a historic building

7 Baltic Sea Science Center

Discover Sweden's diverse underwater environments here **(left)**, from coastal archipelago to open sea. Don't miss the school-themed fish tank.

8 Giant Dala Horse Statue

At the heart of Skansen, atop Orsa Hill, is a giant red statue of a Dala horse – a traditional toy dating from the 17th century that has become a symbol of Sweden.

9 Skansen Glassworks

Skilled glass-blowers use traditional tools to create unique designs.

SPECIAL EVENTS

All of Sweden's major festivals are celebrated here – Midsummer, the traditional Christmas market, and New Year's Eve. Sing-a-long in Skansen is a Swedish institution featuring contemporary artists. It is held on Tuesday evenings in summer.

10 Gardens

These gardens **(below)** provide a contextual landscape to the buildings. The Skåne farmstead has a shady garden in keeping with rural southern Sweden, while the town quarters include allotments.

Map of Skansen

6 Cafés and Restaurants

Have a romantic dinner at the Tre Byttor Tavern, savour a classic Swedish smörgåsbord at Solliden or grab a snack from a kiosk. Many visitors bring their own picnics.

NEED TO KNOW

MAP F4 ■ Djurgårdsslätten 49–51 ■ 08 442 80 00 ■ Tram 7; bus 67; ferry from Slussen to Djurgården; hop-on hop-off buses ■ www.skansen.se

Open 10am daily; check website for closing times

Adm 125–220 kr (adults); 60 kr (4–15s); under 4s free; combined Skansen and Aquarium: 225–295 kr (adults); 110 kr (4–15s); under 4s free

■ **Admission prices are at their highest in summer and during special events, and are significantly cheaper in winter.**

■ **Skansen Terrassen, open all year round, offers good-value meals, including a vegetarian option, an à la carte menu and children's dishes.**

TOP 10 Vasamuseet

An impressive warship built between 1626 and 1628, the *Vasa* had a fatal flaw – she was top heavy, with insufficient ballast. She capsized and sank shortly after setting sail on her maiden voyage. In 1961, her remarkably intact hull was raised after 333 years under water. She is now preserved under controlled conditions to prevent decay, along with a host of fascinating artifacts recovered during the salvage operation. The museum also tells the story of the *Vasa* and her recovery. Models and reconstructions bring it all to life, while getting up close to the vessel is a unique experience.

1 Lion Figurehead

The many lion sculptures reflect the fact that King Gustav II Adolf, who commissioned the building of the vessel, was known as the Lion of the North. The crowning glory is the 3-m- (10-ft-) long lion figurehead at the bow.

2 Objects

Several objects were recovered from the ship and sea bed. The upper gun deck alone yielded a chest of personal items – a felt hat, sewing tools, a comb, gloves, a keg, a wooden spoon, coins and some smaller belongings.

3 Upper Deck

Skilled carpenters restored the destroyed upper deck **(left)** in the 1990s. While entire new parts were needed to complete it, original timber has been used as much as possible.

4 Skeletons

The skeletons of around 15 sailors were found during the salvage operation. The exhibition Face to Face includes a fantasy "meeting" with some of the individuals from the *Vasa* in a film, and through a series of six facial reconstructions.

5 Gun Deck

The *Vasa* was a warship armed with powerful artillery; there were 48 24-pounder cast-iron guns **(above)** on both its upper and lower gun decks.

NEED TO KNOW

MAP Q4 ■ Galärvarvsvägen 14 ■ 08 519 548 00 ■ www.vasamuseet.se/en

Open Jun–end Aug: 8:30am–6pm daily; Sep–end May: 10am–5pm daily (to 8pm Wed), closed 23–25 Dec

Adm 150 kr; under 19s free

- **The museum offers information sheets and audioguides in many languages. Guided tours are available in English – times vary, check website.**
- **Museum can be reached by tram, bus and ferry. Check website for up-to-date information.**
- **A restaurant serves both light refreshments and hot and cold food.**
- **Stop at the gift shop to buy souvenirs.**

THE SINKING

On 10 August 1628, the *Vasa* sat ready for sea, moored below the Royal Palace. For the first few hundred metres, she was pulled along using anchors. As she began to move on her own, four of her ten sails were set. As soon as she caught the wind, she heeled over twice. Water rushed in through the open gunports and she sank after sailing barely 1,300 m (4,265 ft). An estimated 30 of the 150 to 200 people on board died. She sank due to insufficient ballast to balance the cannons and rigging, causing the hull to ride too high.

6 Stern

Many of the ship's 500 sculptures were centred on the stern **(above)**, a symbol of Sweden's might. Although it was badly damaged, it has been carefully restored to reveal the ornamentation.

Vasamuseet Floorplan

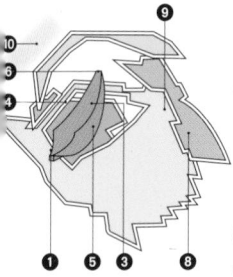

Key to Floorplan

- Ground floor
- Second floor
- Third floor
- Fourth floor

7 Sculptures

Several sculptures, including one of cherubs around the royal emblem, show how Gustav II Adolf wanted the world to see himself and Sweden.

8 Cannons

Most of the 64 cannons **(above)** were salvaged in the 17th century, using a diving bell for the recovery operation. The museum displays three of the largest, cast in bronze and weighing 1.2 tons each.

9 Film

The rediscovery of the sunken *Vasa* by a maverick archaeologist and its painstaking raising from the seabed between 1959–61 is the subject of a short film shown in the museum.

10 The Vasa Museum Garden

The garden cultivates plants that would have been vital to the health of those aboard; rambling hops, harvested in late summer, would flavour and conserve beer.

TOP 10 Stockholm Archipelago

Stretching from Stockholm's outskirts to 60 km (37 miles) further east, the Stockholm Archipelago (Skärgård) is one of the most spectacular in the world. Consisting of around 30,000 islands and islets, it changes in character further east towards the open sea. Around 150 islands are inhabited; others are little more than bare rock. The archipelago comes alive in summer, when it is possible to take anything from a 25-minute boat hop to Fjäderholmarna to a two-hour-plus journey further afield.

1 Siaröfortet

Built as part of a defence line against naval forces, Siaröfortet is a warren of underground rooms, including barracks and a kitchen, plus guns embedded in the rock. It was decommissioned in the 1960s and has now been restored as a museum.

2 Sandhamn

The archipelago's yachting centre, Sandhamn's harbour **(below)** is busy in summer – reflected in its lively party atmosphere. However, it also has a superb beach, Trouville, which is perfect for families.

3 Fjäderholmarna

An ideal day trip for those who want a taste of the archipelago without a long journey, this island **(above)** can be reached from May to October by frequent boats from Nybroplan or Slussen.

4 Norröra

The inspiration for Astrid Lindgren's TV series *Life on Seacrow Island*, Norröra has not changed a lot since 1964.

Map of Stockholm Archipelago

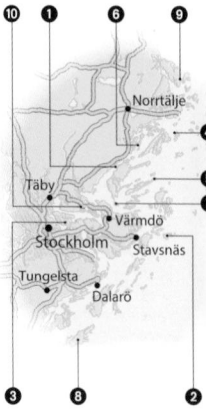

5 Finnhamn

A group of islands in the outer archipelago, Finnhamn is accessible by boat all year round, and its hostel welcomes guests from late spring till autumn. It also has an organic farm.

6 Ängsö Nationalpark

A national park since 1909, this is the place to experience a slice of old Sweden, much as it was hundreds of years ago. There is a signposted network of walking trails.

7 Grinda

One of the most popular archipelago destinations, Grinda offers a range of accommodation. The island's restaurants are highly popular in summer.

RURAL ISLANDS

Gällnö, a long-standing agricultural community, has striking landscapes of fields, meadows and glacial rocks. Själbottna, part of the Östra Lagnö nature reserve, is an excellent place to pitch a tent for the night and has secluded spots for bathing. Landsort, on the southernmost part of Öja, is home to the country's oldest functioning lighthouse. Rödlöga, which means "bathed in red", is a granite island on the archipelago's outer reaches, the last stop for regular boat services.

NEED TO KNOW

- Ferry from Stockholm to the archipelago: Waxholmsbolaget
- 08 600 10 00
- www.waxholmsbolaget.se

- **Most of the islands listed on these pages are only accessible by scheduled boat services, so plan a trip carefully. Transport to many of the islands is very limited, sometimes to only one boat a day.**
- **Catering facilities on the islands range from top-quality restaurants in the more popular destinations to simple cafés or kiosks, or in some remote instances, nothing at all. There are plenty of spots to enjoy a secluded picnic.**

8 Utö

In the southern part of the archipelago, Utö **(above)** offers outdoor activities such as canoeing and cycling. It has pretty beaches, good lodging options and cafés.

9 Arholma

The last outpost in the northern archipelago, Arholma has a beautiful landscape, most of which is a nature reserve. Sights here include a Midsummer pole in the form of a fully rigged mast and the Arholma watch beacon **(right)**, built in 1768 and now an art gallery.

10 Vaxholm

The archipelago's main town, Vaxholm is watched over by an old fortress and has many restaurants and cafés along the waterfront, where boats arrive. The island is also accessible by bus 670 from Stockholm.

Things to Do

1 Beaches and Swimming

The water might be quite chilly, but everyone goes swimming and paddling in the sea to cool off during the warmer summer months. The popular island of Grinda is about an hour away by ferry from central Stockholm, or you can simply take bus 428X from Slussen to Björkvik for swimming and sandy beaches with fine views across the water.

2 Farm Stays

www.ostanviksgard.se

Stay overnight at Östanviks Gård, a thriving archipelago farm, on the island of Nämdö, which dates back to the 16th century, or buy produce directly from its little shop.

3 Kayaking

www.ingmarso.se

At Ingmarsö, visitors can rent single or double kayaks, or take a group tour around the nearby islands with a guide. The boat trip from Stockholm to Ingmarsö takes two and a half hours to the south jetty.

Children kayaking at Ingmarsö

Lunch at the Artipelag Museum

4 Day Trip with Lunch at an Archipelago Restaurant

www.visitskargarden.se

Numerous day trip packages take away the hassle of organizing travel and food, especially as tables in many restaurants can be fully booked in the high season. Visit the website for a choice of day trips.

5 Cottage Rentals

www.skargardsstugor.se

Experience island life at close quarters by renting a cottage for a weekend or longer. Some islands have limited shopping facilities and often no alcohol store, so visitors may need to bring most or all their supplies with them. Stockholm Archipelago Vacation Rentals has cottages to rent in the archipelago.

6 Boat Hiking

www.waxholmsbolaget.se/visitor/archipelago-traffic/island-hopping

The Island Hopping pass is valid for five days from the first journey and can be used on all Waxholmsbolaget boats. The pass comes with a map and suggested itineraries, including where to arrive at an island, hike across it and leave by ferry to continue on to another island.

7 Fishing

Going fishing with a hand tackle is allowed without a licence everywhere in the archipelago. For more serious fishing, hire a guide, many of whom offer boats, equipment, life vests and overalls. There are organized fishing trips from time to time – check at the tourist offices.

8 Winter Boat Trips

www.stromma.se

Enjoy the peace and tranquillity of the archipelago amid snow and ice with a winter island-hopping cruise. Strömma offers a three-hour brunch cruise, departing at noon every Saturday and Sunday, aboard the 70-year-old *S/S Stockholm*.

Waxholmsbolaget steamboat

9 Steamboat Tours

Beautifully maintained veteran steamboats operate in high summer. Take one of the scheduled services for a day trip to Vaxholm or to one of the other islands such as Grinda. Or, choose a day or evening cruise with the option of lunch or dinner.

GETTING THERE AND AROUND

Boat timetables are available in printed form from all SL travel offices *(see p110)* and from tourist centres. Schedules can be complicated – some boats only sail on certain days – so check carefully; visitors taking a day trip must make sure they can get back. The fastest are the Cinderella ships, which cut journey times to the middle and outer archipelago. It is also possible to reach a lot of islands by bus, followed by a shorter boat trip – connections are given in the timetable. Winter boat schedules are limited. The main boat operator is Waxholmsbolaget *(see p107)* – its website, available in both Swedish and English, contains useful timetables and journey planners.

10 Camping

With the right of public access, anyone can pitch a tent in most open spaces. However, if you want fresh water and toilets, there are many designated camping spots, either free of charge, or for a small fee.

Camping in the archipelago

PRO MUNDI VITA

TOP 10 Stadshuset

The imposing red-brick City Hall is one of Stockholm's major landmarks, dominating the northern shore of Riddarfjärden bay. Completed in 1923, it is built in the National Romantic style, with the austere Nordic Gothic building juxtaposed with northern Italian features. Now containing government offices, the building can be viewed by guided tour only, but visitors can stroll at leisure through the courtyard and gardens, as well as climb the tower.

1 The Golden Hall

More than 18 million glass and gold mosaic fragments, the work of local artist Einar Forseth (1892–1988), adorn the impressive Golden Hall's walls **(right)**. They depict Swedish history using a Byzantine-inspired style.

2 Statues

The beautiful gardens are filled with many statues. The steps to the water are flanked by two of Carl Eldh's sculptures: *The Song* and *The Dance*. On a 20-m (65-ft) pillar in the south-east corner is *Engelbrekt the Freedom Fighter* by Christian Eriksson.

3 The Blue Hall

The venue for the Nobel Banquet, the Blue Hall was meant to have its bricks painted blue, but the architect Ragnar Östberg was so taken with the natural red that he had a last-minute change of heart.

Stadshuset Floorplan

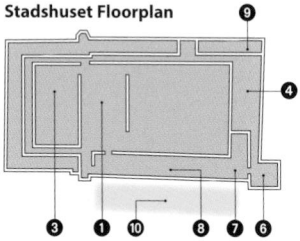

4 Council Chamber

Stockholm's local councillors meet in this magnificent chamber **(left)**, known as the Rådsalen in Swedish, every third Monday. The 19-m- (62-ft-) high ceiling takes inspiration from the Swedish Viking Age. The public viewing gallery can accommodate about 200 spectators.

Previous pages *The Royal Chapel nave at the Royal Palace (Kungliga Slottet)*

6 Tower

Climb to the top of the 106-m- (348-ft-) tall tower **(left)** for superb views over the city from the open-air terrace. Visit the Tower Museum, located in the middle of the tower. A lift goes halfway to the top.

7 Oval Room

Weddings and civil partnerships are solemnized here. The walls are covered with a series of five 300-year-old tapestries woven in France.

NOBEL BANQUET

The Nobel Banquet is held in Stadshuset's Blue Hall annually on 10 December, after the Nobel Prize ceremony. Among the 1,300 guests are members of the Swedish Royal family and 250 students. There are lighthearted speeches by each of the Nobel Laureates, and ceremonial toasts. The banquet is also broadcast live on Swedish TV and radio.

5 Three Crowns

Sweden's heraldic symbol and national emblem of the three gold crowns – Tre Kronor – sits on top of the tower.

8 Prince's Gallery

On the south side of Stadshuset are French windows offering a wonderful view of Lake Mälaren and Södermalm; the gallery's opposite wall **(above)** reflects this in a fresco called *Stockholm's Shores* (1922) painted by Prince Eugen, brother of King Gustav V.

9 Cellar Restaurant

Dine in Stadshuskällaren *(see p75)*, the cellar restaurant. It offers a wide range of classic Swedish dishes such as meatballs or marinated salmon.

10 Gardens

The south-facing garden **(below)**, popular with sightseers and sunbathers, sits between Lake Mälaren and the Stadshuset building.

NEED TO KNOW

MAP K4 ■ Hantverkargatan 1 ■ 08 508 29 058 ■ Open 8am–4:30pm Mon–Fri (Tower: open May–Sep) ■ www.stockholm.se/CityHall

Stadshuskällaren: www.stadshuskallarensthlm.se

■ **To take the best photos of Stadshuset, walk eastwards to the path on the central railway bridge, Centralbron. You can snap some great shots from across the water.**

■ **Adjacent to the hall, towards the street of Norr Mälarstrand, a kiosk sells ice creams and hot and cold drinks.**

■ **Groups of more than 10 require reservations.**

TOP 10 ★ Drottningholm

The superbly preserved Drottningholm Palace and its grounds date from the 17th and 18th centuries, inspired by French models such as Versailles. On UNESCO's World Heritage list since 1991, the palace is the Swedish royal family's permanent home. Rooms in the southern wing are reserved for this purpose; the rest of the palace and grounds are open to the public. The grounds have trees dating from the palace's heyday as a royal court. It was abandoned, then fell into decay in the mid-19th century, but, after a six-year-long renovation from 1907, it began to be reused by the royal court.

1 Queen Lovisa Ulrika's Library

Decorated in the 18th century by Jean Eric Rehn for the queen, the library includes paintings of historic events such as the crossing of the Great Belt in Denmark in 1658.

2 The Nature Path

Close to the Chinese Pavilion, the nature path is a peaceful walk for anyone who wants to learn more about the flora and fauna and cultural history linked to the island of Lovön where Drottningholm is situated. The path is also signposted in Braille.

3 Court Theatre

This theatre, which is still preserved in its original condition, dates from 1766. Each summer it hosts around 30 performances, mainly 18th-century opera and ballet in period costume.

4 Queen Hedvig Eleonora's State Bedroom

Created over 15 years, the queen's ornate state bedroom **(below)** was the heart of the state reception suite in the 17th century.

5 Baroque Garden

The oldest part of the gardens **(below)** is laid out in a formal French style. Many of the statues were taken from cities captured by the Swedes, including the Wallenstein Palace in Prague.

6 Chinese Pavilion

At the time when this pavilion was built, as a surprise gift from King Adolf Fredrik to his wife Lovisa Ulrika in 1753, there was great interest in all things Chinese – the style is typically 18th-century Chinese.

7 Guards' Tent

Built in 1781 to serve as quarters for the dragoons of Gustav III, the Guards' Tent **(above)** resembles a tent in a Turkish army camp. The history of Drottningholm's Royal Guard is described in one of the rooms.

8 Staircase

Large statues of nine muses are placed on the balustrade, and *trompe-l'oeil* paintings by Johan Sylvius adorn the walls of the stair hall.

9 Studio of Evert Lundquist

The studio **(below)** is a museum housing oil paintings, drawings and engravings by Evert Lundquist (1904–94).

ROYAL RESIDENCE

Drottningholm Palace became the official royal residence in 1981, after falling in and out of favour with successive Swedish monarchs throughout its roughly 300-year lifetime up to that point. Often used as a summer residence during its first 150 years, it was abandoned throughout the reign of Charles XIV John (1818–44) and fell into decay, before being gradually repaired and restored under Oscar I, Oscar II and Gustav V.

10 Drottningholm by Boat

From May to October, steamships cruise on Lake Mälaren from the city centre to the palace. Boats depart from Stadshusbron, right beside the City Hall. Visit the palace's website for departures and fares.

NEED TO KNOW

MAP G2 ■ 08 402 62 80 ■ www.kungahuset.se ■ Ferry from Stockholm *(see pp106–7)*

Open Jan–Mar: noon–3:30pm Sat & Sun; Apr: 11am–3:30pm daily; May–Sep: 10am–5pm daily; Oct: 10am–4pm Tue–Sun; Nov–Dec: 10am–4pm Sat & Sun

Adm 130 kr (adults); 65 kr (7–17s & students). Combination ticket includes the Chinese Pavilion: 200 kr (adults), 100 kr (7–17s & students).

■ **Drottningholm is a great day out for budget travellers – the gardens and Guards' Tent are all free and offer lots to see and do.**

■ **The visitor centre provides information and sells tickets. There is also a gift shop and restaurant.**

Top 10 ★ The Royal Palace (Kungliga Slottet)

Stunning rooms – more than 600 of them – and priceless jewels and artifacts are just some of the highlights of the Royal Palace. As one of the largest royal palaces still in use – it is the workplace of the monarchy – this is deservedly one of the city's showpiece attractions. Reminiscent of a Roman Baroque palazzo, it was designed by architect Nicodemus Tessin to replace the old Tre Kronor castle that burned down in 1697. Containing five different museums, the palace is guarded by the Royal Guard.

1 Tre Kronor Museum

Built around the remains of a 12th-century defensive wall and housed in vaults from the 16th and 17th centuries, this museum takes visitors **(below)** back to the original Tre Kronor palace, most of which was destroyed in a fire in 1697.

2 Bernadotte Apartments

The king receives foreign dignitaries in the East Octagonal Cabinet – the rooms are still furnished as they were in the mid-18th century. Do not miss the impressive library **(left)**.

3 Royal Chapel

The beautifully decorated chapel holds mass for employees of the Royal Court every Sunday; all staff can attend. It also holds classical music concerts.

4 Gustav III's Museum of Antiquities

First opened in 1794, this museum includes a collection of statues bought by King Gustav III on a visit to Italy in 1783.

5 Hall of State

The highlight of the royal apartments, the Hall of State features the silver throne of Queen Kristina, who became queen-elect at the age of just five, later abdicating aged 28.

6 Guest Apartments

These beautiful rooms includes the Meleager Salon, a mix of Rococo and Gustavian styles. There is also a cabinet piano in mahogany with white-marble pilasters.

8 The Royal Guard

Drawn from the Swedish armed forces, the Royal Guard **(left)** has been protecting the palace since 1523. The Changing of the Guard takes place daily at midday, sometimes with music.

7 State Apartments

The royal family has lived at Drottningholm *(see pp24–5)* since 1981, but earlier inhabitants have left their mark here. The White Sea Ballroom **(above)** epitomizes the height of 18th-century elegance.

NEED TO KNOW

MAP M4 ■ Slottsbacken, Gamla Stan ■ 08 402 61 30 (weekdays 9am–noon) ■ Tunnelbana: Gamla Stan, Kungsträdgården; buses 2, 76 ■ www.kungahuset.se

Open Oct–Apr: 10am–4pm daily; May–Jun & Sep: 10am–5pm daily; Jul–Aug: 9am–5pm daily

Royal Apartments: 160 kr (adults); 80 kr (7–18s & students); under 7s free

■ **The entry fee to the palace includes a 45-minute guided tour.**

■ **For details regarding visiting the different museums, check the Kungahuset website.**

PALACE HISTORY

Kungliga Slottet was originally a 13th-century fortress, but evolved into a palace in the 17th century. Work to develop it began in 1692 under architect Nicodemus Tessin the Younger, but, in 1697, a fire destroyed most of the palace. Tessin submitted drawings for the new palace – the plan was for it to be built in about five years. However, the royal family was not able to move back in until 1754.

9 Karl XI's Gallery

This magnificent room is the palace's banqueting hall; official and state dinners, and a dinner in honour of Nobel Prize winners are all held here.

10 Treasury

The state regalia, including King Erik XIV's crown, are kept in deep cellar vaults. The 1696 silver font is still used at royal baptisms.

Royal Palace Floorplan

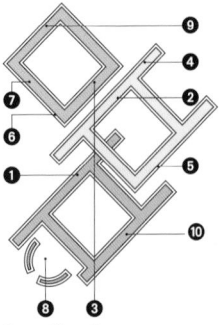

Key to Floorplan

- Ground floor
- First floor
- Second floor

TOP 10 Gröna Lund

Founded in 1883, Gröna Lund (the Green Grove), is Sweden's oldest amusement park – a mix of modern thrills and old-fashioned charm in an excellent waterside setting. Suitable for all ages, it offers a wide range of rides and attractions. Thrillseekers will love the park's seven roller coasters, but there are also more sedate rides – carousels with original 19th-century fittings and traditional sideshows. Gröna Lund is also a major concert venue, attracting big-name acts over the years, such as The Who, Bob Marley and Lady Gaga.

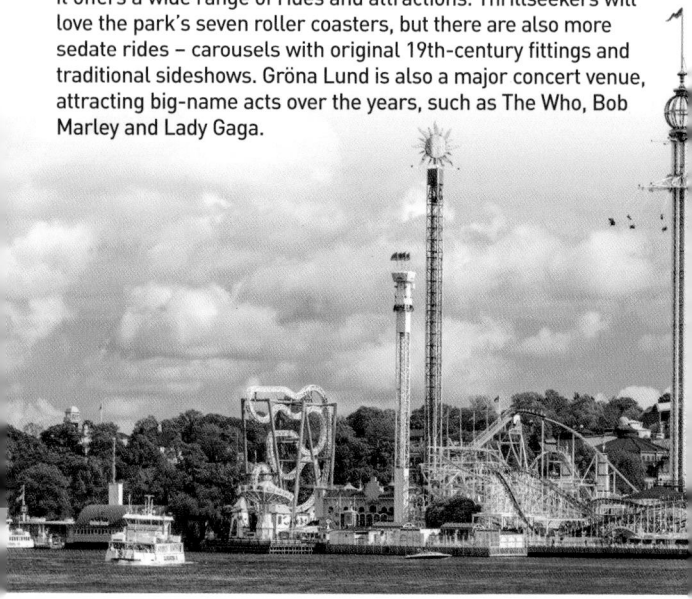

1 Roller Coasters

There are eight roller coasters at Gröna Lund, including the Jetline, which reaches speeds of 90 kmph (56 mph), and the wooden Twister by the waterfront. The Ladybird can be enjoyed by all ages.

2 Stages

There is both a large and small stage here, and some concerts are included in a day ticket, but it costs more for major events. A *guldkortet*, or gold card, provides unlimited admission, including to concerts, over a year.

Map of Gröna Lund

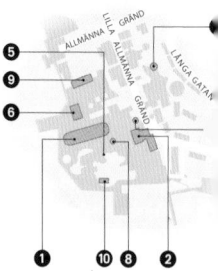

3 The Old Carousel

The carousel **(left)** dates all the way back to 1892. Choose from riding lovable pigs, proud lions, traditional white horses or even a giraffe.

4 Free Fall Towers

One of the highest free fall towers in Europe at 80 m (262 ft), this ride is for intense thrill-seekers only, and definitely only those with no fear of heights. To see the city of Stockholm, take the Free Fall Tilt, which tilts before it falls, for an added thrill.

Gröna Lund rides

5 Blå Tåget

Classic house rides **(below)**, dating back to 1935, were revamped with advance technology to scare and haunt the riders.

6 Fun House

Lustiga Huset, or Fun House, is a genuine original from the 1920s with wacky rooms and wobbly bridges, and has been the inspiration and design for several fun houses in the world.

7 Restaurants and Bars

There are five restaurants and bars, plus kiosks selling traditional Swedish waffles and ice cream. Other outlets specialize in Thai and Mexican food, falafels, kebabs and burgers.

HISTORY

In the early days, Gröna Lund's main attraction was a carousel moved by a horse. Founder Jacob Schultheis's son, Gustav Nilsson, laid the foundations of the modern attraction in the 1920s, adding rides and building the first concert stage. The park's popularity surged in the 1960s when it became Sweden's major music venue. But it remains true to its origins; most of the buildings date from the 19th century.

8 Eclipse

One of the latest additions to the park, this gravity-defying ride **(right)** takes exhilaration to new heights. At 122 m (400 ft) it is the highest StarFlyer in the world, and offers a 360-degree view of the capital.

9 Tunnel of Love

This tunnel takes you through a magical fairytale world decked with twinkling lights. Hold hands, steal a kiss or just enjoy its charm.

10 Flying Carpet

A wild and scary ride is what you would expect from a real flying carpet and this does not disappoint. Sit on the edge for an exciting ride.

NEED TO KNOW

MAP R6 ■ Lilla Allmänna gränd 9 ■ 010 708 91 00 ■ Tram 7; bus 67; ferry from Slussen to Djurgården ■ www.gronalund.com

Open Apr–Sep, check website calendar for full details, as opening times vary according to the time of year

■ **Euros (notes only) are accepted at all the entrance and ticket booths, souvenir and photo shops, as well as kiosks and stands. The highest note accepted is €50, and change is given in kronor – the service centre exchanges euros for kronor.**

■ **Step into the ABBA musical at *Mamma Mia! The Party* at Tyrol by Gröna Lund. Enjoy a three-course Mediterranean meal while musicians perform *Waterloo, SOS, Mamma Mia,* etc. Booking in advance is essential.**

TOP 10 Nordiska Museet

A monument to Swedish cultural history, Nordiska Museet has exhibits that document everyday life in Sweden from the 16th century to the present. Created by Artur Hazelius, the founder of Skansen, Nordiska Museet is housed in an imposing Renaissance-style building and the entrance features a huge statue of King Gustav Vasa. With over 1.5 million exhibits to see, visitors are spoiled for choice here – yet, much of the museum reflects simple everyday life in Sweden through the ages.

1 Traditions

When do Swedes eat *semlor*, cream buns with marzipan? Where did traditional Christmas celebrations originate? What are the origins of the Midsummer pole? The answers to these and other questions can be found in this exhibition, which covers festivals throughout the year.

4 Capturing the Moment

On display are some rare and well-known photographs **(left)** by Kerstin Bernhard (1914–2004), best known for her fashion and food photography.

5 Table Settings

Re-creations of table settings from the 16th to 20th centuries highlight customs about food and drink, and how cutlery and drinking vessels have developed.

2 Main Hall

A fitting entrance to the museum, the hall has a monumental statue of King Gustav Vasa (1523–60; **right**) at its centre. It was carved by Carl Milles from oak in 1924.

3 Dolls' Houses

There are 15 dolls' houses, which reflect the styles and home decor of different periods in history.

6 Sámi Life in Sweden

The Sámi are the Nordic countries' only, and Europe's northernmost, Indigenous people. This exhibition examines their traditional way of life and influences on Swedish culture.

AUGUST STRINDBERG

Famous author, painter, photographer and theatrical director, Strindberg (1849–1912) took a personal interest in the Nordiska Museet project and contributed ideas. After his death, much of his work was given to the museum.

Nordiska Museet façade

8 Swedish Folk Art in the 18th and 19th Centuries

Rural folk art blossomed in the 18th and 19th centuries – craftspeople passed on their skills from one generation to the next. Indeed, its heritage lives on today as a big influence on Swedish design **(above)**.

9 Strindberg Collection

The museum owns the largest single collection of August Strindberg's paintings in the world. Sixteen of these are on display, along with some photographs taken by Strindberg and several of his original manuscripts.

7 Small Objects 1700–1900

From 1872, Artur Hazelius began gathering the items that make up this collection. As he wandered through rural Sweden, Hazelius acquired a complete range of household objects.

Nordiska Museet Floorplan

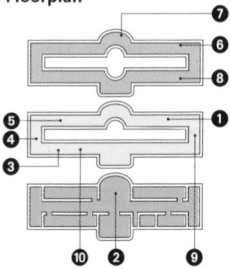

Key to Floorplan

- First floor
- Second floor
- Third floor

10 My 1950's

This exhibition **(below)** looks at clothing from the 1950s, when fashion was influenced by the economy and flow of ideas. It offers an insight into everyday wear and the finest finery worn by wealthy fashionistas and women in rural areas.

NEED TO KNOW

MAP Q4

- Djurgårdsvägen 6–16 ■ 08 519 546 00
- Tram 7; buses 67, 69 & 76 ■ www.nordiskamuseet.se

Open 10am–5pm daily (Sep–May: to 8pm Wed)

Adm 140 kr (adults); under 18s free

- **Borrow an audio guide and follow a map to see the best of the museum in an hour. The guide explores the galleries, as well as the museum's history and architecture. Guides are available in several languages.**
- **The museum restaurant serves hot, traditional, Swedish-style meals.**

TOP 10 Historiska Museet

The Swedish History Museum, opened in 1943, focuses on early civilization in Sweden, especially from the initial traces of human societies to the Middle Ages. It is particularly renowned for its Gold Room. Built in reinforced concrete to ensure security, the room showcases 52 kg (114 lbs) of gold objects, as well as over 250 kg (551 lbs) of silver items, mainly from the Bronze Age to the Middle Ages. Other sections take a fresh approach of presenting historical trends and events up to the present through engaging displays.

1 Medieval Massacre

With the help of unique objects, such as this rusted armour **(above)**, the horrifying story of the battle between the farmers of Gotland and the well-trained soldiers of the Danish army is told.

2 Maria from Viklau

Wood has long been a popular material for sculptures in Sweden. This richly gilded and colourful figure of the Madonna without child is one of the best-preserved examples of early medieval Swedish sculpture. This piece originates from Viklau Church on the island of Gotland, back in the late 1100s.

3 Gold Room

Priceless artifacts in the Gold Room **(below)** include Bronze Age jewellery and a Medieval reliquary, demonstrating the skills of craftsmen of that era.

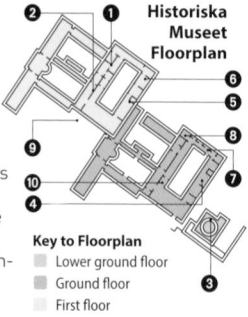

4 Vikings

The embellished swords of the Vikings are on display here, but shattering many of the myths surrounding the Vikings are objects **(above)** from everyday life that prove that they mostly led a peaceful existence as traders.

5 Medieval Art

This unique exhibition displays decorative ecclesiastical items, such as ornate altarpieces, wood carvings and religious art, from the 12th to the 16th centuries.

6 History Unfolds

Created by different artists, History Unfolds is a fascinating exhibition detailing Sweden's history and how it has influenced Swedish society. All the artwork is inspired by the museum's collections.

7 Alunda Elk

This carved stone moose head was used as a ceremonial axe; animals such as moose and bear were symbols of the gods in the Stone Age.

8 Bronze Age Finds

Priceless artifacts have been uncovered after 3,000 years, often by amateurs. These include human figures in bronze **(left)** found in Skåne, a gold bowl discovered by an army lieutenant and his daughter out for a walk in 1847, and a gold cup unearthed by a widow in 1859, for which she earned the equivalent of six months' wages.

BRONZE DOORS

Historiska Museet's bronze doors are called Historiens Portar or 'The Gates of History'. They took Swedish sculptor Bror Marklund 13 years to make and weigh around one ton. Their engravings depict the history of Sweden from the Stone Age to the Middle Ages with one exception – a 1950s pilsner bottle on the right-hand door, a tribute to the workers who built the museum.

9 History of Sweden

Discover Swedish history from the 11th century to the present in a series of displays based around events in the lives of famous and lesser-known historic persons.

10 The Woman from Barum

This moving exhibit features the skeleton of a 155-cm- (5-ft-) tall woman who lived in the Stone Age **(above)**. It tells us that she died at around 45 years of age and that she had borne many children. She was discovered in the 1930s, buried in a pit.

NEED TO KNOW

MAP Q2 ■ Narvavägen 13–17 ■ 08 519 556 00 ■ Tram 7 to Djurgårdsbron; buses 67, 69 & 76; Tunnelbana to Karlaplan ■ www.historiska.se

Open Sep–May: 11am–5pm Tue & Thu–Sun (to 8pm Wed), closed Mon; Jun–Aug: 10am–5pm Tue–Sun; closed Mon & for Midsummer

■ **Informative audio guides are available in different languages for many of the exhibitions for a small charge.**

■ **Children of all ages are well catered for here with a number of activities, including a history trail from Viking times through to the Middle Ages, guided tours, special audio guides and themed weekends.**

■ **Café Rosengården (same opening hours as the museum) serves lunch, snacks and drinks.**

TOP 10 Hagaparken

A vast green area north of the city, the historic Haga is one of Stockholm's most beloved parks. Created in the late 18th century by King Gustav III, its natural "English" style was a reaction to formal Baroque designs. Some 26,000 trees were originally planted, interspersed with lawns and winding pathways. Buildings erected between 1786 and 1793 include the Chinese Pavilion, Copper Tents and the Temple of Echo. It is the perfect getaway in any season – in summer, it is popular for picnics, sunbathing or just taking it easy.

1 Stora Pelousen

Epitomizing the park's English character, the *Pelouse* – French for lawn – has been a recreational destination for Stockholmers for over 200 years. It is a popular sunbathing spot in summer, while skiers take over in winter.

2 Cafés

The Copper Tents have a coffee shop and picnic room. A small café in the park serves freshly baked cinnamon buns, coffee and snacks.

3 Echo Temple

A Swedish national monument, this temple **(left)** was built in 1790 as a summer dining room for King Gustav III. It is an outdoor museum and a popular wedding venue.

4 Copper Tents

The tents' façades are adorned with painted copper plates **(above)**, giving the illusion of a sultan's encampment. The middle tent houses the park museum.

NEED TO KNOW

MAP G2 ■ 4 km (2.5 miles) N of Stockholm ■ 08 27 42 52 ■ Bus 57 from Slussen, Sergels Torg and various stops in the city (direction Karolinska Sjnkhuset (Hospital) to Haga Norra or Haga Södra); Tunnelbana to Odenplan then bus 515 ■ www.kungahuset.se

Park: open year round

Fjärilshuset: open Apr–Sep: 10am–5pm daily (Oct–Mar: to 3pm Tue–Sun); adm: 175 kr (adults), 90 kr (4–15s)

Haga Parkmuseum: open Apr–Sep: 10am–4pm Sat & Sun

Gustav III's Pavilion: open May–Aug: Sat & Sun by guided tour only; tour in English at 3pm

■ **Download a free English audio guide to the park as an MP3 from www.onspotstory.com.**

■ **There are many secluded spots to enjoy a picnic.**

Map of Hagaparken

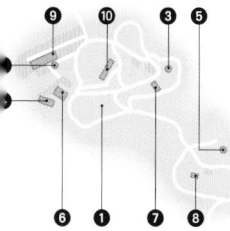

6 Haga Parkmuseum

The original model of the palace that King Gustav III was having built at the time of his assassination in 1792, and which never made it to completion, is on display in the museum. It also includes information about the people associated with Haga, such as the poet Carl Michael Bellman.

LOCAL PERSONALITY

Much of local composer, musician and poet Carl Michael Bellman's (1740–95) writing is associated with the park, although he only wrote one song about Hagaparken. His popular song *Fjäriln vingad syns på Haga* describes the beauty of the park. It can be recited by heart by many Swedes.

5 Chinese Pagoda

This open octagonal structure was built in 1787. Its tented roof was adorned with dragon heads with bells. It was repaired in 1974, when new dragons made of toughened plastic replaced the former decaying oak ones.

7 Gustav III's Pavilion

Dating from 1787, this pretty little palace **(above)** has light, airy interiors, inspired by the antique Roman villas of Pompeii, which had just been discovered.

8 Turkish Pavilion

Completed in 1788, this pavilion was used by King Gustav III to hold meetings with his closest advisors. There are plans to restore the original furnishings, which have been traced in the royal palaces.

9 Fjärilshuset

Even in the depths of the harsh Swedish winter, the daytime temperature at the, butterfly and bird house never drops below 25° C (77° F). The house provides a habitat for butterflies **(below)**, tropical insects, spiders and parrots.

10 Haga Ruins

Work started on the foundations and cellars of a grand palace in 1786 but ceased when Gustav III was murdered. The palace **(left)** was never completed.

The Top 10 of Everything

Brick Gothic interior of Storkyrkan, Stockholm's cathedral

Moments in History	38
Churches	40
Museums and Galleries	42
Parks and Gardens	44
Off the Beaten Path	46
Children's Attractions	48
Pubs and Bars	50
Cafés	52
Restaurants	54
Places to Shop for Swedish Design	56
Stockholm for Free	58
Festivals and Events	60

Top 10 Moments in History

1 1252: Foundation of Stockholm

Stockholm is first mentioned in records from the 13th century. The name probably originates from the Swedish words *stock* (log) and *holm* (islet) – for the logs used to build the Gamla Stan area *(see p84–91)*, and particularly the fortress built by the ruler Birger Jarl in 1252. This protected the passage from Lake Mälaren to the Baltic, vital for trade with Germans. It burned down in 1697, and the present-day Royal Palace was built on its site.

2 1520: Stockholm Bloodbath

The culmination of a long Danish campaign to take control of Sweden, the Stockholm Bloodbath saw around 80–90 people, mainly clergy and members of the nobility who supported the influential Sture party, being executed one by one at Stortorget, outside the Tre Kronor palace. The event led to severe opposition to Danish rule.

Portrait of Gustav Vasa

3 1523: King Gustav Vasa

Having managed to avoid the Stockholm Bloodbath, nobleman Gustav Vasa led a rebellion against Danish rule; it ended with him being crowned king on 6 June 1523 – Sweden's National Day. Sweden was united under his 37-year rule, an era seen as the birth of modern Sweden, during which it also became a Protestant country.

4 1792: Murder of Gustav III

Gustav III was a patron of the arts, literature and theatre; he founded prestigious academies, such as the Swedish Academy and the Royal Opera, and initiated reform programmes. But opposition to his absolute powers and expensive foreign policy cost him his life – in 1792, he was shot during a masked ball at Stockholm's Opera House.

Etching of the Stockholm Bloodbath

5 1871: Industrialization

The completion of a railway to both the north and the south helped Stockholm begin its rapid industrial progress. In 1876, Lars Magnus Ericsson founded the Ericsson phone company in the capital, leading the way for Stockholm to establish an extensive phone network.

6 1912: Summer Olympics

The Stockholm Olympic Stadium, built for the 1912 Olympics, is still used as a major sports and concert venue. The games were known as the "Swedish masterpiece" because they were so well organized, and included the first such use of electronic timing and PA systems.

7 1936: Rise of the Social Democrats

Dominating Swedish politics from 1936 until the 1980s, the Social Democrats established the modern welfare state and shaped the 20th-century development of Stockholm. Poverty was virtually eradicated in the 1930s and 1940s, and almost the entire country was electrified and connected by new roads.

8 1965: Housing Modernization Programme

A construction project, known as the Million Programme, succeeded in its aim to build over a million new homes, but received mixed reactions – the main criticism being that many of the blocks were uninspiring.

Former Prime Minister Olof Palme

9 1986: Olof Palme's Assassination

The killing of popular Prime Minister Olof Palme in central Stockholm on 28 February 1986 was shocking. Palme was shot while returning from the cinema; the murderer remained a mystery until 2020, when prosecutors announced that it was Stig Engström, a Swedish graphic designer.

10 21st Century

Present-day Sweden is regarded as having a robust economy and seen as a leader in many technological fields as well as design and style. A strong promoter of equal rights, Sweden consistently ranks high in the OECD Better Life Index and the Global Sustainability Index.

TOP 10 INFLUENTIAL FIGURES

Monument to Astrid Lindgren

1 Carl Linneaus (1707–78)
Responsible for the classification of living things, botanist Linneaus travelled extensively to find different species.

2 Alfred Nobel (1833–96)
This scientist and inventor held 355 different patents, and used his fortune to found the Nobel Prize.

3 August Strindberg (1849–1912)
Author of *The Red Room*, the father of modern Swedish literature was also a playwright, painter and photographer.

4 Tage Erlander (1901–85)
Prime Minister of Sweden for an uninterrupted and unprecedented 23 years, Erlander's tenure is a record for parliamentary democracies.

5 Dag Hammarskjöld (1905–61)
Hammarskjöld was the UN Secretary General from 1953 until his untimely death in a plane crash.

6 Greta Garbo (1905–90)
A Hollywood legend, actress Garbo retired at just 43 years of age.

7 Astrid Lindgren (1907–2002)
An internationally acclaimed author, whose *Pippi Longstocking* series was translated into around 100 languages.

8 Ingmar Bergman (1918–2007)
Director and writer of over 60 films, he was described by Woody Allen as "probably the greatest film artist".

9 Olof Palme (1927–86)
Palme hugely influenced domestic and international politics, and was twice the Prime Minister.

10 Greta Thunburg (b 2003)
Thunburg started a global strike from school to raise awareness about the climate crisis in September 2019. Since then, she has become a world renowned environmental activist.

Top 10 Churches

1 Tyska Kyrkan

This church *(see p88)* is a reminder that German merchants dominated the Old Town in the Middle Ages. Also called St Gertrude's Church after the patron saint of travellers, it was founded in 1571, and includes a gallery built in 1672 for German royals. The pulpit from 1660 is in ebony and alabaster.

Stained-glass window, Tyska Kyrkan

2 Storkyrkan

Stockholm's cathedral *(see p86)*, with origins dating back to the 13th century, is known for its collection of artistic treasures. The sculpture *St George and the Dragon* by Bernt Notke, from 1489, was created to mark the Battle of Brunkeberg, while the "Sun Dog Painting" of a light phenomenon over Stockholm in 1535 is said to be the oldest colour depiction of the city.

3 Högalidskyrkan

MAP B5 ■ Högalids Kyrkväg ■ 08 616 88 00 ■ Open 10am–5pm daily ■ www.svenskakyrkan.se/hogalid

This National Romantic-style church was completed in 1923. Legend has it that it was financed by two sisters, each more affluent than the other. One of the octagonal towers appears to be taller when viewed from certain angles, though both towers are in fact 84 m (275 ft) high.

4 Gustav Vasa Kyrka

MAP B2 ■ Odenplan ■ 08 508 886 00 ■ Open 11am–6pm Mon–Thu (to 3pm Fri–Sun) ■ www.svenskakyrkan.se/gustafvasa

The Italian Neo-Baroque-style dome of this church dominates Odenplan square. Built in 1906, the church contains Sweden's largest Baroque sculpture, which forms the altar. It was created by court sculptor Burchardt Precht between 1725 and 1731 for the Uppsala Cathedral.

5 Adolf Fredriks Kyrka

MAP L1 ■ Holländargatan 16 ■ 08 20 70 76 ■ Open 1–6pm Mon, 10am–4pm Tue, Wed & Fri–Sun, 10:30am–4pm Thu ■ www.svenskakyrkan.se/adolffredrik

Dating to 1768, this city centre church is built in the shape of a Greek cross with a central dome. The interior includes a memorial sculpture to French philosopher Descartes by Johan Tobias Sergel. The cemetery contains the grave of Prime Minister Olof Palme *(see p39)*.

6 Riddarholmskyrkan

A burial church *(see p85)* for the Swedish royal family since medieval times, this is one of the oldest buildings, dating to the 13th century. More of a museum, the church is open to the public in the summer.

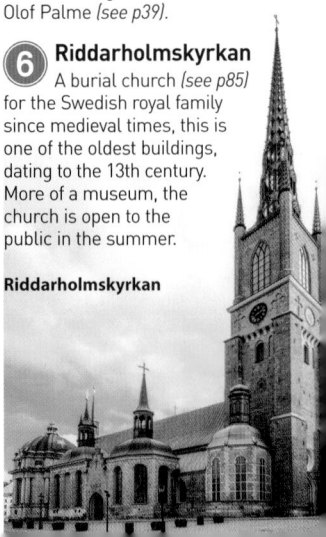

Riddarholmskyrkan

The nave of Sofia Kyrka, showing its National Romantic features

7 Sofia Kyrka

MAP E6 ■ Vitabergsparken ■ 08 615 31 00 ■ Open 9am–5pm Mon–Fri, 10am–5pm Sat & Sun ■ www.svenskakyrkan.se/sofia

Set high up in Vitabergs park, Sofia Kyrka was built in 1906 after Gustaf Hermansson won a contest for its design. The building has National Romantic and Gothic influences.

8 Maria Magdalena Kyrka

MAP M6 ■ Bellmansgatan 13 ■ 08 462 29 40 ■ Open 11am–5pm Mon–Wed, Fri & Sat (to 7pm Thu) ■ www.svenskakyrkan.se/mariamagdalena

Maria Magdalena began as a funeral chapel in the 14th century. The current building, with its pretty yellow spire, was finished in 1763. Famous national poet and singer Evert Taube is buried here.

9 Katarina Kyrka

MAP D5 ■ Högbergsgatan 13 ■ 08 743 68 00 ■ Open 11am–5pm Mon–Sat, 10am–5pm Sun ■ www.svenskakyrkan.se/katarina

Completed in 1695, this church was damaged by fire in 1723 and then burned down almost completely in 1990. It took five years to restore. Its graveyard is the resting place of famous Swedes, including assassinated foreign minister Anna Lindh.

10 Engelbrektskyrkan

MAP D1 ■ Östermalmsgatan 20b ■ 08 406 98 00 ■ Open 11am–3pm Tue–Sun ■ www.svenskakyrkan.se/engelbrekt

Opened in 1914, Engelbrektskyrkan dominates the Lärkstaden area of Östermalm, with its slim tower and the highest nave in Scandinavia supported by eight granite pillars. Its interior features suitably monumental paintings by Olle Hjortzberg.

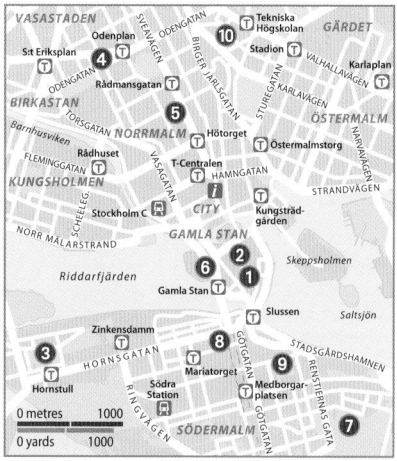

TOP 10 Museums and Galleries

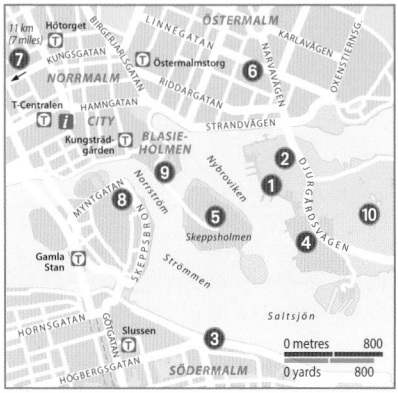

through the ages. The museum is housed in a palatial building on Djurgården island.

3 Fotografiska

Opened in 2010 as a centre for contemporary photography, the gallery *(see p94)* presents four large exhibitions and a vast number of smaller ones annually. Housed in a former industrial Jugend-style building on Stockholm's waterfront, it also has an excellent café-bar.

1 Vasamuseet

The only fully preserved 17th-century warship in the world, the *Vasa*, despite its impressive appearance, sank shortly after setting sail on its maiden voyage in 1628 and was not recovered until 1961. With three masts projecting from the roof, the Vasamuseet *(see pp14–15)* is a unique attraction.

2 Nordiska Museum

Discover Sweden's cultural history in this museum *(see pp30–31)*. Exhibitions on trends and traditions, folk art, textiles and fashion, and furnished rooms reveal life in Sweden

4 ABBA The Museum

Few cultural entities have put Stockholm – and Sweden – on the map like ABBA did in the 1970s and 1980s, when they ruled the global pop charts. See their costumes, gold records and other memorabilia up close, and even try singing along with their 3D holograms at this fun museum *(see p78)* – an essential visit for all ABBA fans.

5 Moderna Museet

This museum *(see p86)* contains one of the world's finest collections of 20th-century art,

Moderna Museum on the waterfront

including works by Picasso, Matisse and Dalí, and makes ongoing acquisitions of recent contemporary art. It also houses photographic art and photography, spanning from the 1840s to the present day.

6 Historiska Museet

The Swedish History Museum *(see pp32–3)* brings civilization alive from the earliest settlements to the Middle Ages. Highlights include exhibits about the Vikings, the life of eight different people from prehistory and the Gold Room.

7 Drottningholm

One of Stockholm's three World Heritage Sites, Drottningholm *(see pp24–5)* comprises a preserved 17th- and 18th-century palace and gardens. The official residence of the Swedish Royal family, it is nevertheless open to the public; an ideal way to visit in summer is a one-hour boat trip across Lake Mälaren from the city direct to the palace.

Drottningholm palace

8 The Royal Palace (Kungliga Slottet)

The world's biggest palace *(see pp26–7)* still used by a head of state, this splendidly appointed building houses the Royal Apartments, the Hall of State, the Treasury and the Tre Kronor Museum. The magnificent rooms range in style from Rococo to Baroque to Gustavian.

Paintings at the Nationalmuseum

9 Nationalmuseum

Paintings and sculptures by great masters such as Rembrandt, Renoir, Rubens, Degas and Gauguin, plus those by Swedish artists Anders Zorn, Agnes de Frumerie, Alice Nordin and Carl Larsson, are housed in Sweden's national gallery *(see p85)*.

10 Skansen

A collection of buildings from across Sweden, including an entire 19th-century town, is the principal attraction at this open-air museum *(see pp12–13)*, concert venue, playground and park. Traditional crafts, including glassblowing, are practised in the workshops, while the Galejan Fairground has old-fashioned toys, funfair rides and a classic car track.

TOP 10 Parks and Gardens

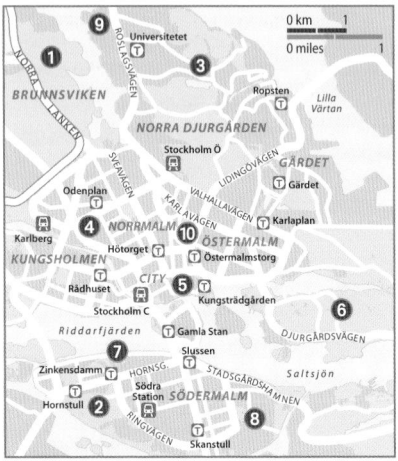

1 Hagaparken

A natural English-style landscaped park, Hagaparken *(see pp34–5)* is loved for its tree-lined avenues, beautiful lawns and royal buildings. A highlight is the tropical butterfly house, which is also home to free-flying birds. Enjoy lunch or a snack inside the blue Copper Tents.

2 Tantolunden

This park *(see p95)* in Södermalm is a popular summer hangout and picnic spot, and includes a few cafés and a mini-golf course. Take a stroll up the hill to enjoy the allotment gardens and good views. There is also a pleasant waterside walk from Tanto to Hornstull.

3 Stora Skuggan

Metro 14 to Stora Skuggan

Located north of the city centre, Stora Skuggan is a popular recreational venue with open areas. In its centre is a youth-run city farm with animals to meet and greet, and a café in an 18th-century building nearby.

4 Vasaparken

Lying between the squares of St Eriksplan and Odenplan, Vasaparken *(see p73)* offers many recreational activities. From November to March there is a mechanically frozen ice rink, keeping the ice good at all times.

5 Kungsträdgården

A lively leafy square very close to the main central shopping areas, Kungsträdgården *(see p66)*, or "King's Garden" has numerous cafés and restaurants along its perimeter. Enjoy the pretty "tunnel" of cherry blossom in the spring, concerts in the summer and ice-skating and a Christmas market in the winter.

Kungsträdgården in bloom

Rosendals Trädgård, Djurgården

6 Djurgården

MAP G4 ■ Tram 7 to Djurgården; get off at Skansen or the terminus at Waldermarsudde

No trip to Stockholm is complete without visiting Djurgården. Not only is it home to several of the city's major museums and attractions – notably Skansen *(see pp12–13)* and Vasamuseet *(see pp14–15)* – but this royal park is an extensive area of greenery with excellent walks and views across the water. Do not miss Rosendals Trädgård *(see p53)*, a garden practising biodynamic agriculture, with an excellent café.

7 Skinnarviksparken

MAP B5

Head to this park on a fine day to picnic with the locals. Featuring a wonderful view across Riddarfjärden and of the city, it is ideal for long summer evenings. The park features Swedish artist Arne Jones' stainless-steel sculpture, *Progression*. There is a small summer café-kiosk and a playground for the kids.

8 Vitabergsparken

MAP E6

This hilly park – whose name means the White Mountains Park – in Södermalm includes an open-air theatre hosting a schedule of free summer concerts and dance performances of all kinds. At its highest point is Sofia Kyrka *(see p41)*, a church inaugurated in 1906. Wooden workmen's cottages line the park, a reminder that this trendy area was once Stockholm's poorest. There is also one of the city's oldest allotment gardens, dating from 1906.

9 Bergianska Trädgården

Frescati, 5 km (3 miles) N of central Stockholm ■ Bus 50 or 540; Tunnelbana Universitetet ■ Conservatory and Orangery: open 11am–5pm daily (winter: to 4pm) ■ Edvard Anderson Conservatory: adm ■ www.bergianska.se

Not far from the pretty Brunnsviken waterside walk, the Bergianska Botanic Garden dates back to the 18th century but shifted to its current location in 1885. Tropical plants bloom in the Orangery and Edvard Anderson Conservatory, which are used for research by Stockholm University. The orangery has a café.

Conservatory, Bergianska Trädgården

10 Humlegården

Oak trees and open lawns characterize this central green oasis *(see p77)* that dates back to the 16th century when it was the Royal Fruit Garden, but has been open to the public since 1869. It includes a large playground and skateboard ramp, and is also home to the National Library of Sweden and a large statue of Carl Linnaeus *(see p39)*. Try the innovative beer ice-cream or the delicious craft beer at Omnipollos Flora, which is situated in the park.

TOP 10 Off the Beaten Path

The elegant pool at the Sturebadet

1 Sturebadet

MAP D2 ■ Sturegallerian ■ Open 6:30am–10pm Mon–Fri, 8:30am–8:30pm Sat & Sun ■ www.sturebadet.se

Dating back to the 19th century and once a haunt of Greta Garbo, plush Sturebadet is one of Stockholm's most upscale swimming pools, gyms and spas only for over-18s. Day passes are available; book in advance.

2 Fjällgatans Kaffestuga

MAP E5 ■ Fjällgatan 37 ■ Open 9am–5pm Mon–Sun ■ Closed Oct–Mar ■ www.fjallgatan.com

Enjoy a coffee or an ice cream with great panoramic views over all of Stockholm at this summer café and terrace, perched on the edge of the cliffs above Södermalm. It faces out towards Gamla Stan, Djurgården, the archipelago and beyond.

3 Hammarbybacken

Hammarby fabriksväg 111 ■ 02 808 80 61 ■ Winter: open 3–10pm Mon & Fri, 10am–10pm Tue–Thu, 9am–6pm Sat & Sun ■ www.skistar.com/hammarbybacken

It sounds unlikely, but downhill skiing is possible in the heart of Stockholm. The artificial slope here offers quality floodlit pistes – covered by snow cannon – for skiers of all ages and abilities winter round. Views from the top stretch to Södermalm.

4 Långholmen

MAP A4 ■ www.langholmen.com

Home to one of Sweden's largest prisons for 100 years, the island of Långholmen, just off the north-western tip of Södermalm, is a lush green oasis perfect for walks, picnics and swimming. The prison is now a hotel/hostel *(see p117)* and museum.

5 The Fishery Teatern

MAP D6 ■ Ringen centrum ■ Open 11am–9pm Mon–Thu (to 10pm Fri & Sat, 8pm Sun)

Famous, award-winning chef Malin Söderström's tiny seafood restaurant, in the Teatern food court, has great dishes such as hearty fish stew, crispy fish with air fried potatoes, and fish tacos with pickled *regnbåge* (trout), along with an impressive range of sparkling wines.

6 Hornstulls Marknad

MAP A5 ■ Hornstulls Strand ■ Open 11am–5pm Sat & Sun ■ Closed Oct–Mar ■ www.hornstullsmarknad.se

Every weekend, the waterfront strip at Hornstull is transformed into an open-air flea market with stalls selling art, antiques, records, crafts and more, and myriad food trucks.

Bric-a-brac stall, Hornstulls Marknad

The vast structure of Ericsson Globe

7 The Sweden Solar System

Ericsson Globe, Globentorget 2 ■ www.swedensolarsystem.se

The world's largest scale model of our solar system has its centre here. The Ericsson Globe *(see p101)* – the world's largest spherical building – represents the Sun and models of the inner planets, from Mercury to Jupiter.

8 Färgfabriken

Lövholmsbrinken 1 ■ Exhibition hall: open 11am–7pm Thu (to 4pm Fri, 5pm Sat & Sun) ■ www.fargfabriken.se

Discover Stockholm's thriving art scene at this exhibition and events space set in a 19th-century paint factory. Exhibitions change regularly, so see the website for details.

9 Vinterviken

Between Gröndal and Aspudden ■ www.vinterviken.com

As well as being a picturesque suburban park surrounding a bay in Lake Mälaren, Vinterviken is also renowned as the site of the former laboratory and factory, where, in the mid-19th century, chemist Alfred Nobel *(see p39)* first produced and tested dynamite. Renovation work in the 1990s transformed the industrial area into the present-day recreational park. One of Nobel's former factory buildings houses the Vinterviken café, restaurant and events venue.

10 Spritmuseum

MAP E4 ■ Djurgårdsvägen 38 ■ 08 121 313 00 ■ Open 10am–5pm Mon–Sat, noon–5pm Sun ■ www.spritmuseum.se

With its state-owned off-licences and history of home-distilling illegal moonshine, Sweden has a somewhat bittersweet relationship with alcoholic spirits. The Spritmuseum is an offbeat shot of history, culture and strong booze. The great restaurant offers creative local cuisine.

Restaurant at the Spritmuseum

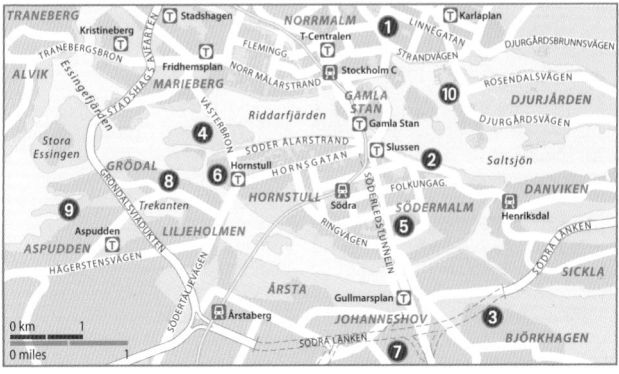

TOP 10 Children's Attractions

Ice-skaters enjoying the winter rink at Kungsträgården in the city centre

1 Junibacken

MAP Q4 ■ Galärvarvsvägen ■ 08 587 230 00 ■ Tram 7; bus 67 ■ Open 10am–5pm daily (Jul–Aug: to 6pm daily) ■ Adm ■ www.junibacken.se

The storybook world of Junibacken opens up like a fantasy adventure. Characters from children's books live around the Storybook Square, while the Story Train transports visitors into the fairytale world of Swedish author Astrid Lindgren.

Kids' story-themed Junibacken

2 Fjäderholmarna

This island *(see p16)* is an ideal kids' day out. Activities include pottery and textile printing, climbing a pirate ship or playing as Vikings. There are play areas and the path along the shoreline is stroller-friendly.

3 Ice-Skating Rinks

Kungsträdgården *(see p66)* in the city centre, Vasaparken *(see p73)* in Vasastan, and Medborgarplatsen *(see p93)* on Södermalm all have outdoor skating rinks in winter. Several ice-hockey rinks are also open to the public. Visit the tourist office for an up-to-date list.

4 The Viking Museum

MAP Q5 ■ Djurgårdsvägen 48 ■ Tram 7; bus 67; ferry from Slussen ■ Open 10am–5pm daily ■ Adm ■ www.thevikingmuseum.com

This museum brings the Viking Age to life and offers an insight into different aspects of the Vikings' culture and day-to-day life. In the 11-minute dramatised ride, Ragnfrids Saga (minimum seven year olds allowed) visitors journey back in time to AD 963.

5 Tekniska museet

MAP G3 ■ Museivägen 7 ■ 08 450 56 00 ■ Open 10am–5pm Thu–Tue (to 8pm Wed) ■ Adm ■ www.tekniskamuseet.se

Sweden's National Museum of Science and Technology is packed with things to entertain and inspire kids, be it making virtual sculptures in the MegaMind Zone or marvelling at Uno Milton's old model railway.

6 Swimming Pools

Hammarby slussväg 20
■ 08 508 402 58 ■ Adm

Eriksdalsbadet, the city's main swimming pool, has adventure pools for children and an outdoor pool in summer. The main adventure pool is comfortably warm and 1.4 m (4.6 ft) deep with two slopes. The outdoor pool is open from late May through to late August.

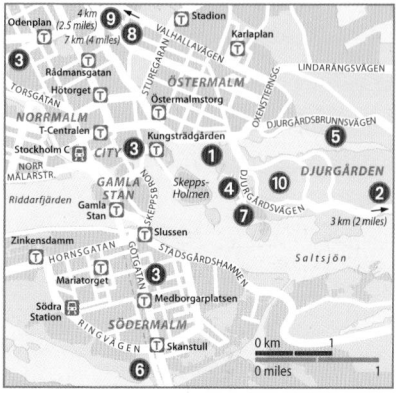

7 Gröna Lund

There are various rides and fairground attractions for children of all ages at this traditional funfair *(see pp28–9)*. Do not miss the Fun House and the various traditional sideshows.

Roller coaster at Gröna Lund

8 Mulle Meck Lekpark

Mönstringsvägen 9, Solna
■ 08 746 10 00 ■ Bus 505 or 540
■ Open daily ■ www.solna.se

Stockholm is child-friendly and kids can play in the Mulle Meck Lekpark, a themed playground, based on George Johansson and Jens Ahlbom's children books. The playground features an airplane hangar, cable cars, a flower maze and an amphitheater. There's also a children's library.

9 Naturhistoriska Riksmuseet

Come face-to-face with dinosaur skeletons while exploring the history of natural life on earth, and also learn about nature in Sweden and the animals found here *(see p99)* by following a discovery trail. There are lots of fun activities to entertain children of all ages, including interactive exhibits. The Cosmonova IMAX cinema shows a variety of educational natural science documentaries.

10 Skansen

Fascinating Skansen *(see pp12–13)* is perfect for a fun day out. The Galejan Fairground has old-fashioned toys, funfair rides such as swings and carousels, and a classic car track. There are also kids' activities in the museum's historical buildings with staff in period costumes teaching interactive lessons on topics including nature, food preparation and farm life.

Exploring the exhibits at Skansen

TOP 10 Pubs and Bars

1 The Flying Elk

One of the best places in the city to sample the latest and best locally and internationally brewed craft beers, The Flying Elk *(see p91)* also does reasonably priced artisanal cuisine. Star chef Björn Frantzén's gastropub is informed both by Swedish tradition and British pub culture.

Elegant interior at Riche

2 Riche

Opened in 1896 with an interior and character inspired by the Café Riche in Paris, Riche *(see p80)* retains an air of elegance and its menu is based around French-Swedish fusion. The media, fashion and art crowd gather here to listen to unconventional DJ sets from Tuesdays to Saturdays. It is also open for breakfast.

3 Snotty Sounds Bar

Tiny, snug and low-lit, Snotty's *(see p96)* is one of the bars of choice for music-lovers. Record sleeves and pictures of punk and indie music legends adorn the walls, and there are DJs most nights of the week. It is packed at peak times, but that is all part of the atmosphere.

4 Morfar Ginko and Pappa Ray Ray

These are two laid-back venues *(see p96)* in one – they are next to each other and under the same ownership. There is great food and a popular cava bar serving tapas from the counter. A secret courtyard is open during the summer.

5 Café Tranan

The cosy bar in the basement of ever-popular restaurant Café Tranan *(see p74)* is second home to Vasastan's music-loving crowd and attracts a good selection of DJs. Friendly and unpretentious, it is crowded on weekends but is also an excellent choice as a place with a bit of life on a weekday evening. The fried herring with mashed potatoes has been a constant on the menu at the café since it opened in 1929.

6 Nya Carnegiebryggeriet

A joint venture between beer brands Brooklyn and Carlsberg, this micro-brewery *(see p103)* and adjoining bar as well as restaurant at Hammarby Sjöstad is popular with craft-beer-loving Stockholmers. Sample one of several unique and delicious brews from Amber Ale to J.A.C.K. IPA, after taking a tour to see how it was made.

7 Kvarnen

One of the few old-style beer halls in the city, Kvarnen *(see p96)* serves beer and traditional Swedish food, including good, traditional lunches, in a retro atmosphere. Its adjoining nightclub-bar is by contrast decorated with bright blue and white

The old-style Kvarnen beer hall

tiles and chrome. Kvarnen is also the pub of Hammarby Football Club and gets crowded and very noisy before home matches.

8 Häktet

Located in a courtyard off busy Hornsgatan, former prison-turned-bar Häktet (Swedish for "detention") has become the kind of place you want to get locked in *(see p96)*. Narrow and winding with a fine kitchen, three bars and a diverse crowd, it is a popular late-night haunt open until 3am Thursday through to Saturday.

9 Akkurat

With over 200 brews available, this Södermalm spot *(see p96)* offers a huge variety of craft beers. You can sample several types of beers here, including some *cuvée* (casks of beer that are stored in the cellar until they reach their prime) and local brews. Akkurat has 23 rotating taps from Swedish brewers and regularly collaborates with Stockholm brands.

10 Landet

Situated next to Telefonplan metro station, bar-restaurant and concert as well as club venue Landet *(see p103)* is so much more than just an unusually hip neighbourhood watering hole. Locals come here for discerningly selected beers, fizz, wines and expertly made cocktails. Keep an eye on listings for the upstairs events space, where up-and-coming musicians perform.

TOP 10 CLUBS AND NIGHTSPOTS

Clubbers at Trädgården

1 Trädgården
Hammarby Slussväg 2
Summer-only club with live bands, dance floor, bars and food stalls.

2 Lilla Hotellbaren
MAP D5 ▪ Folkungagatan 50-52
Lilla hosts a wide range of acts from up-and-coming to top DJs.

3 Debaser
MAP A5 ▪ Hornstulls Strand 4
Club with live music, international DJs, and a restaurant. It also hosts concerts.

4 Café Opera
MAP M3 ▪ Karl XII's Torg
Dance-oriented club in a 19th-century building. Attracts guests of all ages.

5 Sturecompagniet
MAP D2 ▪ Sturegatan 4
Four halls on two levels, each with its own musical style.

6 Spy Bar
MAP M1 ▪ Birger Jarlsgatan 20
Attracts media folk and serious clubbers and plays everything from funk and alternative disco to rock and pop.

7 Solidaritet
MAP M2 ▪ Lästmakargatan 3
Electronic dance music from top Swedish and international DJs.

8 Fasching
MAP C3 ▪ Kungsgatan 63
A classic jazz, soul, reggae and Latin club that attracts all ages.

9 Berns
MAP N3 ▪ Berzelii Park
Huge dining room and bars, an outdoor terrace, plus international DJs.

10 Under Bron
Hammarby Slussväg 2
A mecca for Stockholm's underground clubbing scene every weekend.

Top 10 Cafés

1 Johan & Nyström

Those serious about their coffee will love Direct Trade roasters Johan & Nyström's concept store. They will not only get an unbeatable cup of the black stuff, but they can also learn how to make their own great coffee at home with the in-house training facilities. The shop *(see p96)* also sells specialist coffee-making equipment imported all the way from Japan.

2 Vete-Katten

The "Wheat Cat" *(see p68)* opened in 1928 and still looks like an old-fashioned Swedish café. It offers traditional local cakes with lots of marzipan, and different types of buns. While its front entrance is found on the busy central street of Kungsgatan, it also has a quiet courtyard at the back that is open during the summer.

The exterior of Vete-Katten

3 Sosta

Consistently rated by coffee connoisseurs as one of the best espresso bars *(see p68)* in the city. Most unusually for Sweden, the baristas at this espresso bar are decked out in a uniform of striped ties and blue shirts. The quality of Sosta's coffee is excellent, and, what's more, there is a fine pastry selection. There is outdoor seating in the summer, but it is often hard to find a place.

4 Saturnus

Everything is big at Saturnus *(see p80)*, with steaming bowls of *caffé latte* plus, according to some, the biggest, and among the best, cinnamon buns in town. It also has a wide range of hot food with good lunches and breakfasts – big as well as small. The theme is colourful and French with a New York twist.

5 Sturekatten

One of the most famous cafés and bakeries in Stockholm is the grand old "Sture cat" *(see p80)*, tucked away in an Östermalm apartment building. It has not been redecorated since the early 20th century, and staff in period dress wait on guests who come here to enjoy some of the biggest and best *kanelbulle* (cinnamon buns) to be found in the city.

6 Petite France

Award-winning bakery and café in the best French tradition, hidden on a side street not far from the waterfront of Lake Mälaren,

Petite France *(see p74)* serves great croissants, brioches and French bread. The continental breakfast is a treat here, and they also do lunches.

7 Chokladkoppen

Something of a Stockholm institution, this popular gay-friendly café *(see p90)* on Stortorget – Gamla Stan's central square – is best known for its superior cinnamon buns, and, as the name suggests, big steaming cups of hot chocolate. It is a handy stop-off at which to refuel and break up a busy day's sightseeing.

8 Mellqvist Kaffebar

A favourite haunt of world-famous crime author Stieg Larsson and his alter ego Mikael Blomkvist, the lead character in the thrilling *Millennium* series trilogy, this Södermalm institution *(see p96)* is always busy with artists, students and young families. It serves great coffee and terrific *kardemummabullar* (cardamom buns), and has a lovely outdoor area, complete with heaters.

9 Greasy Spoon

Enjoy breakfast, brunch or lunch with a British twist, from a full English and avocado, bacon or salmon eggs Benedict or eggs pretty much any way you want them. A Bloody Mary is optional. They *(see p96)* do not take advance bookings, so set an alarm nice and early or expect to wait in a queue at peak times.

Brunch offerings at Greasy Spoon

10 Rosendals Trädgård

A summer paradise, these public gardens *(see p80)* showcase organic cultivation to the public. Naturally all food served in the café is organically grown on site, and there is also a bakery and a shop. Grab an outdoor table or take your tray to sit under a tree in the apple orchard during spring and summer. Although pricey, it is exceptionally popular at weekends – choose a weekday to avoid the crowds. Check their website for latest opening times.

Greenhouses with flower shops and a restaurant, Rosendals Trädgård

TOP 10 Restaurants

Sleek and modern Scandinavian design at Matbaren

1 Matbaren

A visit to this award-winning restaurant *(see p91)* in the Grand Hotel is a gastronomic event. The theme is not ostentatious; simplicity combines with great attention to detail. The food is Swedish with global influences on a daily changing menu. Prices match the experience.

2 Rolfs Kök

This popular restaurant *(see p69)* features in the Michelin guide and serves creative Modern Swedish dishes, such as pork confit with cabbage and beer-braised onions. The outstanding wine list perfectly complements the food.

3 Calexico's

An innovative Californian-Mexican cuisine is made with organic ingredients at this restaurant *(see p97)*, adjoining and owned by music venue and club Debaser. Think quesadillas, burritos and tacos packed with ingredients, such as lime, coriander, chilli, hot salsa, avocado, mango and more.

4 Lilla Ego

Award-winning chefs Tom Sjöstedt and Daniel Räms serve sophisticated seasonal dishes, such as fallow deer with Jerusalem artichokes and pork tartare with red beet purée, at this bistro *(see p75)*. The exquisite food, along with the restaurant's friendly neighbourhood vibe, is the reason Lilla Ego is fully booked months in advance.

Wild Turbot and flowers, Gastrologik

5 Gastrologik

The food at Gastrologik *(see p81)* is so of-the-moment fresh that there are no standard menus – the best local ingredients of the day dictate the dishes instead. The 18–20-course tasting menu is a gastronomical journey of Nordic cuisine.

6 Nytorget Urban Deli

In keeping with the trendy SoFo area, Nytorget Urban Deli *(see p97)* has a New York-style atmosphere: it is a restaurant, bar, deli and store all rolled into one. The vibe is unpretentious; families with children will feel at home here.

7 Ekstedt

A star chef famed for his rustic cooking on open fires, Niklas Ekstedt lit the flame under his signature Stockholm restaurant *(see p81)* in 2011, and it has burned brightly ever since. Guests can experience set menus of four or six courses, which can feature anything from dried reindeer to birch-fired wild duck.

8 Meatballs for the People

There are few dishes more synonymous with Sweden than meatballs, and not many restaurants do them better than Meatballs for the People *(see p97)*, with no fewer than 14 different varieties including elk, beef and boar. Enjoy with classic cream sauce and lingonberries or served on top of linguine.

9 Punk Royale

Off-the-wall Punk Royale *(see p97)* is full of mischief, fun, energy and invention. Expect the unexpected here, with dishes such as caviar served with vodka shots and prawn skewers in a plant pot. The set menu promises "over delivery" and "gastronomic decadence".

10 Sturehof

Bustling and cool, this classy seafood restaurant *(see p81)* with an excellent reputation focuses on Swedish-French home cooking – the menu follows the seasons, complemented by a huge wine list.

Kerbside dining at Sturehof

TOP 10 SWEDISH FOOD AND DRINK

Traditional Swedish meatballs

1 Swedish Meatballs
The classic Swedish *köttbullar* are made with beef and served with mashed potato and lingonberry jam.

2 Cinnamon Buns
Kanelbulle, the perfect accompaniment to coffee or tea, is found in almost every café in the city.

3 Smörgåsbord
A spread of different hot and cold dishes that varies according to the event or season.

4 Pytt i Panna
A classic Swedish "hash" based around diced, fried potatoes with meat or a vegetarian meat substitute.

5 Semla
A bun filled with almond paste and whipped cream, traditionally eaten around Shrove Tuesday.

6 Västerbotten Cheese
The king of Swedish cheeses is a hard, salty, cow's milk cheese. Also try some mature Prästost or Grevé.

7 Surströmming
Fermented, tinned, raw herring, eaten in August. Very pungent, so the tin must only be opened outdoors.

8 Cloudberries
Hjortron is a delicacy that flourishes only in cold climates. Cloudberry jam is best enjoyed with ice cream or waffles.

9 Must
Non-alcoholic drink with spices, hops and malt, giving it a sweet, beery taste. Swedes drink it mainly at Christmas and Easter.

10 Swedish Beers
Swedish craft-beer culture is on the up; try a brew from one of Sweden's flourishing microbreweries.

TOP 10 Places to Shop for Swedish Design

1 Granit

MAP D5 ■ Götgatan 31 ■ 08 642 10 68 ■ www.granit.com

Discover clever new ways to arrange, light and decorate the home with the functional and creative homeware from this furnishing shop.

2 Design House Stockholm

MAP D3 ■ Hamngatan 18–20 ■ 08 762 81 19 ■ www.designhousestockholm.com

Browse interior design products, porcelain and clothing by top Swedish designers at this chain's flagship shop at the NK department store.

3 Rodebjer

MAP N2 ■ Smålandsgatan 12 ■ 08 611 01 17 ■ www.rodebjer.com

Swedish designer Carin Rodebjer creates practical and elegant womenswear inspired by Swedish folk attire, 1920s bohemian style and rock bands. She has thrice been named Elle's Fashion Designer of the Year.

4 Swedish Hasbeens

MAP E5 ■ Nytorgsgatan 36a ■ 08 702 01 01 ■ www.swedishhasbeens.com

Head here for women's clogs, handmade using sustainable materials, and based on original Swedish 1970s designs. This is the flagship store of this fashion sensation, in trendy SoFo.

Objects for sale at Designtorget

5 Designtorget

MAP D5 ■ Götgatan 31 ■ 08 644 16 78 ■ www.designtorget.se

Brighten up your life with a smart piece of design from this emporium stocking all kinds of easy-on-the-eye items, primarily by Scandinavian designers. Some well-known brands are stocked, from String shelves to Marianne Westman kitchenware.

6 Svenskt Tenn

MAP E3 ■ Strandvägen 5 ■ 08 670 16 00 ■ www.svenskttenn.se

Swedish-Austrian architect and designer Josef Frank designed the gorgeously patterned and coloured

Bold homeware at Svenskt Tenn

fabrics and furniture sold here. Their waterfront headquarters since 1927 also has a tea room and a studio.

7 Fillipa K

MAP D2 ■ Grev Turegatan 18 ■ 08 545 888 88 ■ www.filippa-k.com

Founded in Stockholm in 1993, Filippa Knutsson's fashion brand is an international success story. The latest collections are on display at this flagship store.

8 Whyred

MAP D3 ■ Mäster Samuelsgatan 3 ■ 08 660 01 70 ■ www.whyred.com

Designer Roland Hjort's colourful clothing for men and women combines clean lines, neat shapes and quirky details, and is influenced by music and art as much as fashion. Located in plush Östermalm, this is Whyred's flagship store.

Scandi design pieces at Grandpa

9 Grandpa

MAP A3 ■ Södermannagatan 21 ■ 08 643 60 81 ■ www.grandpa.se

The quality of the product is always more important than the strength of the brand at Grandpa, which stocks a hand-picked selection of fashion, interior and design items.

10 Acne Studios

MAP D3 ■ Norrmalmstorg 2 ■ 08 611 64 11 ■ www.acnestudios.com

From the 100 pairs of jeans made by co-founder Jonny Johansson in 1997 and given out to friends, Acne Studios has become an internationally successful fashion house designing both men's and women's collections.

TOP 10 SOUVENIRS

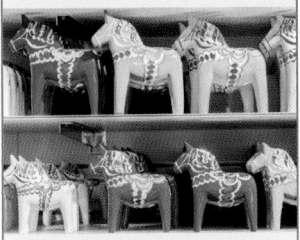

Brightly coloured Dala horses

1 Dala Horse
Classic Swedish ornaments, these delightful handmade and painted wooden horses come in various sizes.

2 String Pocket Shelving
Take home a suitcase-friendly sized set of one the most iconic of Swedish home furnishings.

3 Fjällräven Backpack
Famous for its fox logo, Fjällräven has been making durable and functional outdoor gear since 1960.

4 Sandqvist Backpack
Classic-looking, uncomplicated and functional backpacks made with stylish fabric. These and the leather bags have distinct Swedish heritage.

5 Trull Chopping Board
This chopping board, inspired by Lisa Larson's iconic porcelain feline, makes kitchen work more fun.

6 Ballograf Pens
These sleek, retro-style beauties come with a lifetime guarantee and contain archive-proof ink.

7 Grasshopper Floor Lamp
Designed by Greta Magnusson Grossman in 1948, this lamp, which comprises a tilted tripod, looks like its insect namesake.

8 Acne Jeans
Stockholm's most famous denim export offers cool, comfortable jeans.

9 Tretorn Rainboots
Designed for Swedish climate, Tretorn's waterproof footwear comes in a range of colours and sizes.

10 Berså Coffee Set
Stig Lindberg's famous floral cup and saucer design made by Gustavsbergs Porslinsfabrik of Sweden. The design has been popular since 1961.

TOP 10 Stockholm for Free

1 Guided Tours of the Swedish Parliament

MAP D4 ■ Helgeandsholmen ■ 08 786 40 00 ■ Open mid-Sep–Jun ■ English tours: 1:30pm Sat & Sun ■ www.riksdagen.se

Take a free guided tour of the Swedish parliament building, the Riksdag. Learn about the work and history of the building and find out what is happening in the parliament today.

2 Art in the Underground

Stockholm's Tunnelbana metro system is known as "the world's longest art gallery". Many stations contain artworks, from sculptures and paintings to video installations, all of them free to view. Some stations are artworks in their entirety – such as Solna Centrum, where the raw bedrock of the ceiling is dramatically painted fiery red.

3 Clubbing for Free

Some Stockholm nightclubs and late-night bars offer free entry before a certain hour, typically midnight or sometimes earlier. Debaser *(see p51)* is particularly well known for this – there may even be a free concert included in the bargain, too.

4 Drottningholm Gardens

At the sprawling royal residency of Drottningholm *(see pp24–5)* it is free to explore the beautifully manicured Baroque gardens and the Guard's Tent – more than enough for a morning or afternoon's visit.

Swimmers on Långholmen Canal

5 Take a Swim

Stockholm's waterways are not only beautiful to look at, but they are also so clean that swimming is possible right in the middle of town. On warm days, beaches, jetties and cliffs are packed with bathers.

6 Museums for Free

Many of Stockholm's best museums are free to enter. These include Moderna Museet *(see p86)*, National Museum *(see p43)*, Medelhavsmuseet *(see p66)* among several others.

7 Contemporary Art and Design

Like many of the museums, several contemporary art galleries and exhibitions spaces are free to enter. For example Bonniers Konsthall *(see p72)* and ArkDes centre for architecture and design *(see p88)*.

Beautiful gardens at Drottningholm

8 Explore the Royal Palace Vaults at the Livrustkammaren

MAP D4 ■ Slottsbacken 3 ■ 08 402 30 30 ■ Open 11am–5pm Tue–Sun (to 8pm Thu) ■ Closed Mon ■ www.livrustkammaren.se

Housed in spectacular vaults beneath the Royal Palace *(see pp26–7)*, the Livrustkammaren (Royal Armoury) is the oldest museum in Sweden. It contains arms and armour, robes from royal weddings and coronations and even blood-stained garments worn by royals at their death.

9 Camping on the Archipelago

Allemansrätten enshrines in Swedish law everyone's right to roam and to pitch a tent on most public and private land, making wild camping a great way to explore the Stockholm Archipelago *(see pp16–19)*. Facilities such as fresh water and toilets are available for free or at a small price at some designated camping spots.

10 Concerts and Festivals for Free

Fritz's Corner: www.fritzscorner.se ■ Popaganda: www.popaganda.se

Discover the Stockholm music scene which has produced many world-renowned acts at free shows and concerts staged at Fritz's Corner and the free annual festival Popaganda at Parkteatern.

TOP 10 BUDGET TIPS

Flea market, Blasieholmstorg

1 Look out for local *loppis*, or affordable flea markets in the city. They can be great for finding bargain Scandi design gems.

2 Walking is a great way to explore the city. Central Stockholm is compact and very pretty, so try to walk around as much as possible.

3 An SL Access card *(see p106)* includes trips on the Djurgården *(see p45)* ferries. It is great for city views from the water.

4 Save money on transport by hiring a City Bike *(see p107)* and using Stockholm's handy cycle lanes.

5 Many restaurants and cafés do a very reasonably priced all-inclusive midday deal, known as a *dagens* lunch.

6 Pack a picnic and head for one of Stockholm's many parks *(see p44–5)* such as Haganparken and Tantoluden or beaches, or the archipelago.

7 Know your alcohol pricing: spirits and cocktails are particularly expensive in Sweden. As in all Scandinavian countries, most locals buy their own drinks, rather than rounds.

8 Party like a Swede and save your money by having a pre-party before heading on a night out.

9 For 295 kr, the *guldkortet* or gold card ticket grants daily free admission to Gröna Lund *(see p28–9)* amusement park. Bear in mind that you will need a separate ticket to attend the summer concerts (Aug–Sep).

10 In winter, spend an evening ice skating for free on frozen Lake Mälaren if the ice is thick enough.

Top 10 Festivals and Events

Participants in Stockholm Pride

1 Stockholm Fashion Week

www.fashionweek.se

The Swedish Fashion Council stages fashion events each year – January/February and August see the major fashion weeks. Other activities during the season include exhibitions, trade fairs and press events.

2 Stockholm Marathon

www.stockholmmarathon.se

Attracting runners from around the world, this marathon takes place on the last Saturday in May or the first in June, and ends in the Olympic Stadium.

3 Stockholm Bauhaus Athletics

www.diamondleague-stockholm.com

The largest annual sporting event in Sweden, this is an international track and field event held at the end of May. Taking place at the 1912 Olympic Stadium, it is part of the International Association of Athletics Federations' Diamond League – the world's foremost one-day athletic meeting circuit.

4 Stockholm Pride

www.stockholmpride.org

The Pride Parade, with over 50,000 participants, is the highlight of the week-long pride festival held at the end of July or beginning of August. The parade is a celebration of human rights and openness; other events include Pride Park, featuring concerts and stalls.

Stockholm Culture Festival

5 Stockholm Culture Festival

www.kulturfestivalen.stockholm.se

Held in August, this festival hosts performances and acts such as dance, music and mime on streets, squares and stages throughout the centre. There is a mini children's festival where kids can dance, sing and listen to stories.

6 Midnattsloppet

www.midnattsloppet.com

The "Midnight Race" is run over 10 km (6 miles) or 5 km (3 miles) by 24,000 runners from around 9:30pm in Södermalm in mid-August; people run well into the night. There are 9 starting groups, ensuring that all ability levels are catered for, from the serious to those in outrageous fancy dress.

7 Popaganda

www.popaganda.se

Stockholm's biggest pop festival is held at Eriksdalsbadet's outdoor baths *(see p49)* over two days at the end of August and focuses on indie pop with a mix of well-established and newer artists.

8 Stockholm Jazz Festival

www.stockholmjazz.se

One of the oldest festivals in Sweden and one of the biggest events in Stockholm, this jazz event takes place in mid-October. Attracting thousands of music lovers, this 10-day festival hosts around 160 concerts at 36 different venues all around the city.

Visitors at Stockholm Jazz Festival

9 Stockholm International Film Festival

www.stockholmfilmfestival.se

Inaugurated in 1990, this two-week-long event in mid-November hosts film screenings all around the city, with an emphasis on new and upcoming, local and international directors. Other highlights through the year include a smaller, five-night outdoor film festival in August.

10 Nobel Day

On 10 December, which is the anniversary of Alfred Nobel's death, the Nobel Prize is awarded in Stockholm in Physics, Chemistry, Medicine, Literature and Economics. After the award ceremony, a widely telecast banquet with 1,300 guests is held in the Stadshuset *(see pp22–3)*.

TOP 10 NATIONAL HOLIDAYS AND CELEBRATIONS

1 Easter
Traditions include egg painting and consumption of sweets and chocolate hidden in paper eggs.

2 Walpurgis Night, 30 April
A traditional spring festival, Valborg is marked with bonfires and parties.

3 International Workers' Day, 1 May
A national holiday marked by the Social Democratic party and labour groups marching in the city centre.

4 Ascension Day, June
Since this falls on a Thursday, many workers take a *klämdag* (a day off) on Friday for a long weekend.

5 National Day, 6 June
A public holiday since 2005, this day marks the date of King Gustav Vasa's ascension to the throne.

6 Midsummer's Eve, June
One of the year's biggest holidays, on the Friday closest to 21 June. Skansen is a great place to join in the summer solstice celebrations.

7 Crayfish Season, August
Always popular, crayfish parties involve shelling the fish by hand and drinking plenty of schnapps.

8 Lucia, 13 December
White-robed girls sing traditional Christmas songs in candlelit processions at schools, churches and workplaces; saffron buns are eaten.

9 Christmas, 24–26 December
Families gather on Christmas Eve to celebrate with a *julbord*, the Christmas equivalent of a smörgåsbord.

10 New Year's Eve, 31 December
Locals spill out onto the streets a few minutes before midnight to enjoy fireworks displays around the city.

Crayfish, crispbread and schnapps

Stockholm Area by Area

Stortorget, the oldest square in Stockholm, bordered by colourful buildings

Norrmalm and City	**64**
Kungsholmen and Vasastan	**70**
Östermalm and Djurgården	**76**
Gamla Stan, Skeppsholmen and Blasieholmen	**84**
Södermalm	**92**
Further Afield	**98**

TOP 10 Norrmalm and City

Glass obelisk, Sergels Torg

Considered the central part of town and known as the "City", much of Norrmalm was laid out in the 1960s and 1970s, when a great many of its 18th-century buildings were demolished and replaced with modern high-rise blocks – a move that many people still think was hasty and ill-considered. Despite the controversy, Norrmalm is one of the city's busiest areas. The modern pedestrian streets are famous for affordable shopping, with many large and trendy stores. Of these, Åhléns City is the largest department store in Sweden, while NK is the most exclusive. The district also has some pleasant squares and the ever-popular Kungsträdgården, an outdoor space where there is always something going on.

NORRMALM AND CITY

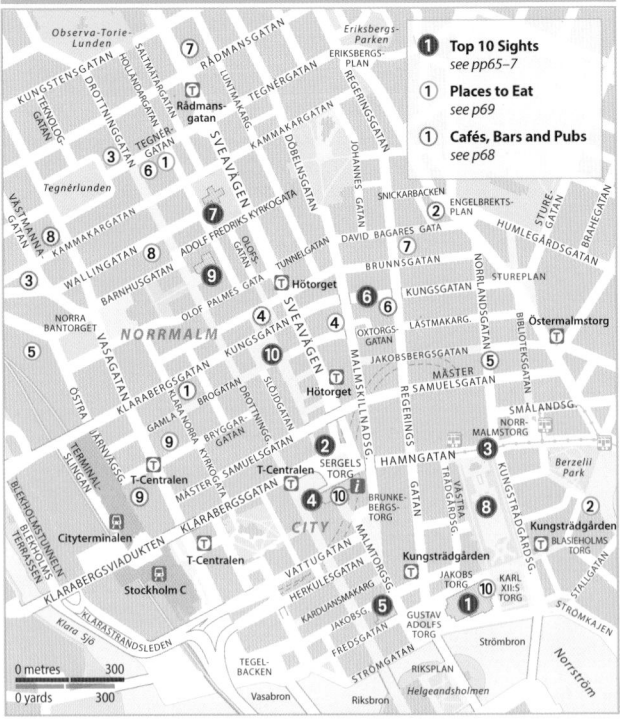

Kungliga Operan auditorium

1 Kungliga Operan

MAP M4 ■ Gustav Adolf Torg 2 ■ 08 791 44 00 ■ www.operan.se

The Royal Swedish Opera is the country's national stage for opera and ballet. Some productions are performed in their original language such as English, German or Italian (with Swedish subtitles). From August to May there are guided tours in English most Saturdays. Take a peek backstage, visit the Royal Suite and look down into the orchestra pit.

2 Sergels Torg

MAP L3

Although not the most beautiful square in Stockholm, Sergels Torg has become an iconic landmark. It is the central hub of the city and home to the T-Centralen Tunnelbana station, where the red and green lines intersect with the blue. The square was designed in the 1960s as part of the modernization of the city centre. It is known for its checkerboard pedestrian area, which is frequently a venue for public demonstrations and street performances. Its highlight, a glass obelisk, is lit up at night.

3 Hamngatan

MAP M3

Stretching from Sergels Torg to Berzelii Park, Hamngatan is one of Stockholm's top shopping streets. It is home to the classic NK department store, trendy Gallerian and the flagship H&M store. Trams on the number 7 line roll down Hamngatan to Djurgården via Norrmalmstorg. This is also where heritage trams leave for Djurgården *(see pp76–81)*. Norrmalmstorg is the site of the 1973 bank robbery that coined the term "Stockholm Syndrome", in which hostages start to sympathize with their captors.

4 Kulturhuset

MAP L3 ■ Sergels Torg ■ 08 508 315 08 ■ Open for events only; check website for programme ■ www.kulturhuset.stockholm.se

This cultural centre was designed by architect Peter Celsing as a "cultural living room". It hosts photographic and art exhibitions, films, theatre and much more. Concerts are held indoors, and, in summer, on the rooftop terrace with great views over the city. There is a café and a children's library, and the Stockholm Visitor Center is located inside.

Kulturhuset on Sergels Torg

Greek busts in the Medelhavsmuseet

5 Medelhavsmuseet

MAP M4 ■ Fredsgatan 2 ■ 010 456 12 98 ■ Open 11am–8pm Tue–Fri (to 5pm Sat & Sun) ■ Adm ■ www.varldskulturmuseerna.se/medelhavsmuseet ■ Bagdad Café: open 11:30am–2pm Mon (to 8pm Tue–Fri), noon–5pm Sat & Sun; Jun–Aug: closed Mon

The Museum of Mediterranean and Near East Antiquities has a collection of ancient and historical relics from the region. The Egyptian exhibition includes mummies, sarcophagi and other ancient burial finds. The Near East and Islamic collections showcase Islamic art from the 7th century onwards. The Cyprus collection has objects excavated by the Swedish Cyprus expedition of 1927–31. There is a restaurant called Bagdad Café.

6 Kungsgatan

MAP M2

"King's Street" was built in 1904–5 to connect Kungsholmen, Norrmalm and Östermalm. It is notable for its two "skyscrapers", Kungstornen, built in 1924–5, and clearly modelled on the Lower Manhattan skyscrapers of that era – they were the first of their kind in Europe. Kungsgatan is a lively shopping street, with many fashion, household and electrical stores, particularly on its eastern end between Hötorget and Stureplan as well as the Rigoletto cinema, dating from 1939.

7 Olof Palme's Plaque and Grave

MAP L1

At the junction of Sveavägen and Tunnelgatan there is a memorial plaque at the spot where Swedish Prime Minister Olof Palme was assassinated on 28 February 1986. People often lay flowers here, particularly on the anniversary of his death. The street to the west was renamed Olof Palmes Gata in his honour. Palme is buried in the nearby Adolf Fredriks Kyrka *(see p40)*, his grave marked by a simple headstone.

8 Kungsträdgården

MAP M3

One of the most popular meeting places in the city, the "King's Garden" *(see p44)* is a hive of activity throughout the year. In winter, it hosts a charming Christmas market and is one of the city's most popular venues for ice-skating; during the summer, it is a great place simply to relax. Open-air concerts and other events are held throughout

Cherry blossoms, Kungsträdgården

the year. A park redevelopment planted 285 linden trees, which replaced old and sick elm trees, and new pavilions with cafés, bars and restaurants.

9 Centralbadet

MAP L1 ■ Drottninggatan 88 ■ 08 545 213 00 ■ Open 7am–8:30pm Mon–Fri, 8am–7:30pm Sat & Sun ■ Adm ■ www.centralbadet.se

Located in a beautiful Art Nouveau building from 1904, Centralbadet is a relaxing oasis just off the busy Drottninggatan. A swimming pool, sun roof, gym, bar, restaurant and the baths are just some of the facilities here. There is also a sauna and a wide range of massages, zone therapy and facial treatments.

Swimming pool in the Centralbadet

10 Hötorget

MAP L2

Just off busy Kungsgatan lies cobbled Hötorget (Hay Market) square, a fruit and vegetable market right in the commercial heart of the city. A statue by sculptor Carl Milles stands outside the pale blue Royal Concert Hall (Konserthuset). To the south stands Filmstaden Sergel, one of the largest multiscreen cinemas in Stockholm showing international blockbusters in their original languages. Beneath the cinema is the Hötorgshallen indoor market, with its vast, mouth-watering displays of Swedish and foreign delicacies. To the north of the square is the excellent Kungshallen *(see p66)* food court.

A DAY IN NORRMALM AND CITY

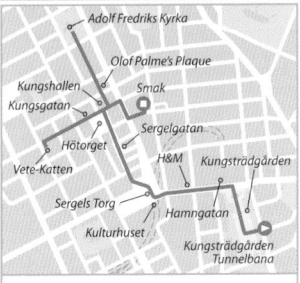

MORNING

Start the day at **Kungsträdgården Tunnelbana** – the terminus of the blue line. It is worth a visit, as it is decorated with relics from 18th-century buildings that were torn down in the 1960s. Take the exit at **Kungsträdgården** park; a stroll northwards through the park leads directly to **Hamngatan** *(see p65)*, where the NK department store sports an iconic revolving neon clock on its roof. Carrying on up Hamngatan, there is both Gallerian and the H&M flagship store, before the street opens out on to **Sergels Torg** *(see p65)*. Pop into **Kulturhuset** *(see p65)* to check out what is on offer and for a coffee at the fifth-floor Café Panorama. Directly off Sergels Torg, pedestrianized Sergelgatan leads to **Hötorget**; grab a light lunch here at either **Hötorgshallen** or **Kungshallen** *(see p68)* foodhalls.

AFTERNOON

Not far from **Hötorget** is **Olof Palme's Plaque**, and his grave in **Adolf Fredriks Kyrka** *(see p40)*, where there is also a memorial to influential French philosopher René Descartes who died in Stockholm in 1649, during his sojourn with Queen Kristina. Spend some time browsing the many shops on **Kungsgatan**, with its 1920s twin towers. From there, walk to **Vete-Katten** *(see p68)* for traditional *fika* (coffee and pastries). From the junction of **Kungsgatan** and **Sveavägen** *(see p71)*, it is not far to **Smak** *(see p69)* for a good-value dinner.

See map on p64 ←

Cafés, Bars and Pubs

An impressive selection of cakes and Swedish pastries at Vete-Katten

1 Vete-Katten

MAP K2 ■ Kungsgatan 55 ■ 08 20 84 05 ■ Open 7:30am–8pm Mon–Fri, 9:30am–7pm Sat & Sun

An old-fashioned café *(see p52)* opened in 1928, the "Wheat Cat" specializes in traditional cakes and buns.

2 Vassa Eggen

MAP D2 ■ Birger Jarlsgatan 29 ■ 08 21 61 69 ■ Open 6:30–10am, 11:30am–2pm & 5:30–11pm Mon–Fri

A popular grill restaurant, this is also a busy nightspot with DJs until late.

3 Waza Restaurant & Brewery

MAP L1 ■ Wallingatan 38 ■ 08 23 00 30

Not only does this pub stock a vast range of beers, it also brews its own.

4 Kungshallen

MAP L2 ■ Kungsgatan 44 ■ Open 9am–11pm Mon–Fri, 11am–11pm Sat, noon–10pm Sun

Hötorget's food court offers a wide choice of international cuisines.

5 Bianchi Café & Cycles

MAP M2 ■ Norrlandsgatan 16 ■ 08 611 21 00 ■ Open 11am–10pm Mon & Tue (to 11pm Wed & Thu, to midnight Fri & Sat, to 5pm Sun)

It is all about traditional Italian quality in this café and bicycle shop serving excellent coffee and snacks.

6 K25 Stockholm

MAP K2 ■ Kungsgatan 25 ■ Open 7:30am–9pm Mon–Fri, 11am–9pm Sat

A budget friendly food hall, where nearly a dozen food vendors sell various specialties.

7 Sosta

MAP L1 ■ Sveavägen 84 ■ 08 612 13 49 ■ Open May–Aug: 8am–6pm Mon–Fri, 10am–5pm Sat

Italian espressos in this café bar *(see p52)* attract rave reviews from Stockholm's coffee aficionados.

8 Pizza Hatt

MAP K1 ■ Upplandsgatan 9 ■ Open 11:30am–2:30pm & 4:30–8:30pm Tue–Fri, 2–8:30pm Sat & Sun

Sourdough pizzas using only fresh ingredients are served at this quirky place. Eat in or take away.

9 Icebar by Icehotel

MAP C3 ■ Nordic C Hotel, Vasaplan 4 ■ 08 50 56 35 20 ■ Open 3pm–midnight Sun–Thu (to 1am Fri & Sat)

Everything from the interior to the glasses are made out of sculpted ice from the arctic Torne River.

10 Café Panorama

MAP L3 ■ Sergels Torg 3 ■ 08 21 10 35 ■ Open 11am–8pm Tue–Fri (to 6pm Sat, to 5pm Sun)

This café *(see p65)* lives up to its name with great views over the city.

See map on p64

Places to Eat

PRICE CATEGORIES

For a three-course meal for one with half a bottle of wine (or equivalent meal), taxes and extra charges.

Ⓚ under 700 kr ⓀⓀ 700–1,000 kr ⓀⓀⓀ over 1,000 kr

1 Supper

MAP K1 ■ Tegnérgatan 37 ■ 08 23 24 24 ■ Open 5pm–late daily ■ ⓀⓀ

Various South American flavours dominate the *platitos* (small plates), which are meant to be shared.

2 Wedholms Fisk

MAP N3 ■ Arsenalsgatan 1 ■ 08 611 78 74 ■ Open 11:30am–2pm & 6pm–11pm Mon, 11:30am–11pm Tue–Fri, 5pm–11pm Sat ■ ⓀⓀⓀ

Traditional, classy fish restaurant offering a great choice of dishes.

3 Grill

MAP C2 ■ Drottninggatan 89 ■ 08 31 45 30 ■ Open 11am–1:30pm & 5pm–late Mon–Fri, 4pm–late Sat, 3pm–late Sun ■ ⓀⓀ

This restaurant serves a variety of wood-fired and charcoal-grilled meats.

4 Smak

MAP L2 ■ Oxtorgsgatan 14 ■ 08 22 09 52 ■ Open 11:30am–2pm & 5pm–midnight Mon–Thu, 11:30am–2pm & 5pm–1am Fri, 5pm–1am Sat ■ ⓀⓀ

The concept is simple but novel at Smak: choose three, five or seven tasting dishes and enjoy the combinations.

5 Cloud Nine Food and Cocktails

MAP J2 ■ Torsgatan 1 ■ 08 653 69 90 ■ Open L: 11am–2pm Mon–Fri; D: 5–11pm Mon–Wed, 5pm–midnight Thu–Sat ■ ⓀⓀ

Relaxed atmosphere and French-Asian cuisine; there is outdoor dining in summer.

6 Rolfs Kök

MAP C2 ■ Tegnérgatan 41 ■ 08 10 16 96 ■ Open 11:30am–1am Mon–Fri, 5pm–1am Sat ■ Ⓚ

Enjoy modern interpretations of classic Swedish dishes here *(see p54)*. Excellent wine list.

7 Nalen Restaurang

MAP M1 ■ Regeringsgatan 74 ■ 08 505 292 01 ■ Open 11am–3pm & 4–11pm Tue–Fri, 5–11pm Sat ■ Ⓚ

Serves classic Swedish food.

8 Tjabba Thai

MAP K1 ■ Wallingatan 7 ■ 08 21 99 88 ■ Open 11am–10pm Mon–Fri, 2–10pm Sat & Sun ■ Ⓚ

Some of the city's best Thai food is served here, including good seafood.

9 Belgobaren

MAP K3 ■ Bryggargatan 12a ■ 08 24 66 40 ■ Open 11am–midnight Mon–Wed (to 1am Thu & Fri), 1pm–1am Sat, 4–11pm Sun ■ Ⓚ

Mussels are served in 10 ways, from classic *moules frites* to those with Asian curry sauces.

10 Operakällarens Bakfickan

MAP M3 ■ Karl XII:s torg ■ 08 676 58 00 ■ Open 11:30am–11pm Mon–Fri, noon–10pm Sat ■ ⓀⓀ

This is a place to enjoy traditional Swedish favourites such as meatballs.

Bar-top seating at Operakällarens Bakfickan

TOP 10 Kungsholmen and Vasastan

Once known as "famine island", with grim industrial businesses and cramped housing, Kungsholmen began to improve in the early 20th century when the Stadshuset, the most prominent building on Stockholm's skyline, was built. Today, the area is known for its buzzy restaurants, bars, cafés and tranquil waterside walks. Nearby Vasastan is home to the lively area around Odengatan, the iconic Stadsbiblioteket and the popular Vasaparken.

Stadshuset as seen from Gamla Stan

KUNGSHOLMEN AND VASASTAN

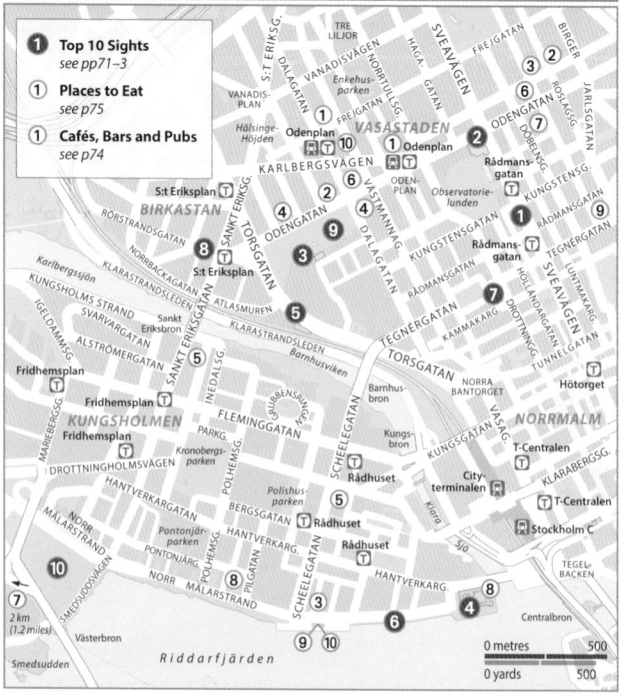

1 Sveavägen

Broad, straight and linking the city centre with Odenplan and beyond, Sveavägen is built like a classic Parisian boulevard. After an unpromising start at Sergels Torg, the street comes into its own after Hötorget – lined with trees and many upmarket shops along with bars and restaurants. Adolf Fredriks Kyrka *(see p40)* and the Stadsbiblioteket are here. After Odenplan, Sveavägen runs on out to the city's northern fringes, just a short walk from Hagaparken *(see pp34–5)*.

2 Stadsbiblioteket

MAP C1 ■ Sveavägen 73 ■ 08 508 310 60 ■ Open 10am–9pm Mon–Thu (to 7pm Fri), 11am–5pm Sat & Sun ■ www.biblioteket.stockholm.se

The Stockholm Public Library was one of the most influential buildings constructed in Stockholm in the early 20th century. Opened in 1928, it was designed by Gunnar Asplund in the so-called Nordic Classicist style. Painted in eye-catching pale orange, its highlight is the central rotunda. Inside, packed bookshelves cover the walls of its tiered balconies, yet with its tall, white ceiling, the rotunda is bright and well lit. It was the first public library in Sweden to adopt the principle of open shelves, where books could be accessed without help from the library staff.

Rooftop of Sven-Harrys Konstmuseum

3 Sven-Harrys Konstmuseum

MAP B2 ■ Eastmansvägen 10 ■ 08 511 600 60 ■ Open 11am–7pm Wed–Fri (to 9pm Thu, 5pm Sat & Sun) ■ www.sven-harrys.se

Building contractor and art collector Sven-Harry Karlson built this spectacular, modern, brass-clad building to house exhibition galleries, an art museum, and restaurants, as well as private apartments. The recessed penthouse is a replica of his own 18th-century mansion and displays his art collection. Do not miss the rooftop sculpture garden.

4 Stadshuset

With its dramatic waterside setting on Riddarfjärden, the City Hall *(see pp22–3)* is visible from far away, and is one of Stockholm's most famous landmarks. It is built from 8 million bricks in the National Romantic style and is home to the municipal council.

Floor-to-ceiling bookcases in the central rotunda of the Stadsbiblioteket

SHOPPING ON KUNGSHOLMEN

Kungsholmen is a great shopping alternative to the city centre crowds. St Eriksgatan and Fleminggatan are the main shopping streets, while Fridhemsgatan and Hantverkargatan are good for second-hand shops.

The modern Bonniers Konsthall

5 Bonniers Konsthall

MAP B2 ■ Torsgatan 19 ■ 08 736 42 48 ■ Open noon–8pm Wed (to 5pm Thu–Sun) ■ Adm ■ www.bonnierskonsthall.se

An unmissable triangular-shaped building designed by local architect Johan Celsing and opened in 2006 contains Bonniers Konsthall, one of Stockholm's leading galleries for both Swedish and international contemporary art. An independent and not-for-profit institution with a mission to increase public consumption of art, it holds free exhibitions that can feature anyone from Turner Prize winners to emerging talent.

6 Norr Mälarstrand

MAP J4

The walk along Norr Mälarstrand is picturesque and popular. Its quay, lined with old ships and houseboats, transforms into a waterside footpath along its western stretch. Either start at Stadshuset or walk towards it from Västerbron (bus 4 stops at Västerbroplan; take the steps down into Rålambshov park to pick up the shoreline walk). Along the way there are several good refreshment and food stops, as well as great views across Riddarfjärden towards Söder.

7 Strindbergsmuseet

MAP K1 ■ Drottninggatan 85 ■ 08 411 91 70 ■ Open noon–4pm Tue–Sun; Jul–Aug: 10am–4pm ■ Adm ■ www.strindbergsmuseet.se

Considered the father of modern Swedish literature, and also a prolific artist, August Strindberg lived in what he called the "Blue Tower" for the last four years of his life. The house is faithfully preserved as he left it, and Strindberg's study, living room and bedroom take visitors back to 1912. There are also many photographic portraits of Strindberg and his family, as well as photographs of places associated with him.

8 Rörstrandsgatan

MAP A2

The street takes its name from the medieval town of Rörstrand, though it is affectionately called "Little Paris" by the residents. Rörstrandsgatan is full of small, interesting stores, which sell everything from British tweed and Italian tiles to handmade chocolates and craft beer. There are also many outdoor cafés and restaurants that give the street a colourful atmosphere during summer. Rörstrandsgatan stretches from S:t Eriksplan and then merges with Karlbergsvägen.

Football pitches in Vasaparken

9 Vasaparken
MAP B2

Vasastan's green lung was developed in the early 20th century as an "open place for free games" – a role it retains today with football pitches, *boules* courts, a landscaped playground and an ice-skating rink in winter. There are also large grassy areas and a popular playground. In 1917, *Arbetaren* (The Worker), a statue by Gottfrid Larsson, was erected to honour the working class. There are numerous kiosks around the park that sell snacks and drinks.

10 Rålambshovsparken
MAP A3

Known locally as "Rålis", this was created as a functional park in 1936, at the same time that Västerbron was built. It is a popular summer haunt with sunbathers, as well as football, *brännboll* (a local form of rounders) and frisbee players. An open-air theatre opened here in 1953.

Norr Mälarstrand on the Kungsholmen waterfront

A DAY IN KUNGSHOLMEN AND VASASTAN

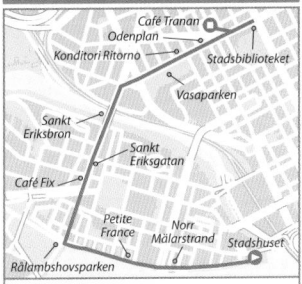

MORNING

Start the day at **Stadshuset** *(see pp22–3)*: tours start at around 10am and the tower is *(open May–Sep: from 9:10am)*. From Stadshuset take the lovely waterside walk along popular **Norr Mälarstrand** – perhaps pop into **Petite France** *(see p74)* for morning coffee and a pastry. Shopping street St Eriksgatan starts at the northeastern corner of **Rålambshovparken** and goes right through the main shopping area of Kungsholmen. As well as taking in the shops, including the mall at Fridhemsplan, grab a light lunch at **Café Fix** *(St Eriksgatan 35)*, which is said to be the oldest café in Stockholm.

AFTERNOON

Crossing St Eriksbron leads to the northern end of St Eriksgatan with its cluster of record stores. From here it is a very short walk to **Vasaparken**, a lovely park to put your feet up with an ice cream in the summer or try ice-skating in winter. Old-fashioned **Konditori Ritorno** *(see p74)* is right opposite the park: cosy and warm in the winter and with a sunny outdoor area in the summer. Head on to Odenplan and pop into the **Stadsbiblioteket** *(see p71)* to admire its impressive rotunda. The Stadsbiblioteket lends more than a million books every year. Round off the day with dinner at **Café Tranan** *(see p74)* – eat in the restaurant or the bar, before enjoying an after-dinner drink with the local crowd.

See map on p70

Cafés, Bars and Pubs

1 Café Tranan

MAP B1 ■ Karlbergsvägen 14 ■ 08 527 281 00 ■ Open 11:30am–11pm Mon–Fri, noon–11pm Sat & Sun

This basement bar *(see p50)* below a restaurant is the perfect place to blend in with the locals.

2 Konditori Ritorno

MAP B2 ■ Odengatan 80–82 ■ 08 32 01 06 ■ Open 7am–10pm Mon–Thu (to 8pm Fri), 8am–6pm Sat, 10am–6pm Sun

Enjoy Swedish filter coffee and delicious cinnamon buns at this retro café and patisserie.

3 Folk & Friends

MAP C1 ■ Norr Mälarstrand 32 ■ Open 4–10pm Tue–Fri (to 7pm Sun), noon–10pm Sat

Enjoy a slice of New Zealand-style pie and some local low-alcoholic craft beers at this friendly pub.

4 Vurma

MAP B2 ■ Gästrikegatan 2 ■ 08 30 62 30 ■ Open 11am–7pm Mon–Fri (to 4pm Sat & Sun)

Choose from a great selection of grilled sandwiches with names such as "Stupid", "Stranger" and "Angel".

5 BrewDog Kungsholmen

MAP A2 ■ Sankt Eriksgatan 56 ■ 08 650 21 10 ■ Open 4pm–midnight Mon–Thu, 3pm–1am Fri & Sat

The Scottish craft-beer brand serves all their hoppy signature brews here, plus select guest pours.

6 Non Solo Bar

MAP C1 ■ Odengatan 34 ■ 08 440 20 82 ■ Open 7am–9pm Mon–Fri, 9am–6pm Sat & Sun

Highly rated for its coffee, this Italian café serves classic food such as pasta, salads and sandwiches.

7 Olssons Skor

MAP C1 ■ Odengatan 41 ■ 08 673 38 00 ■ Open 9pm–3am Wed–Sat

Dark and intimate, this stylish club plays classic electro beats until late.

8 Petite France

MAP B3 ■ John Ericssonsgatan 6 ■ 08 618 28 00 ■ Open 7am–6pm Mon (to 10pm Tue–Sat), 9am–5pm Sun

Entering this café feels *(see p52–3)* like stepping into a French bakery, with bread and pastries to match.

9 Man in the Moon

MAP C2 ■ Tegnérgatan 2c ■ 08 458 95 00 ■ Open 11am–11pm Mon (to midnight Tue–Thu, to 1am Fri & Sat)

This traditional pub with an English feel has a wide range of Swedish craft beers.

10 Orangeriet

MAP B4 ■ Norr Mälarstrand Kajplats 464 ■ 08 505 244 75 ■ Open 11am–11pm Mon–Thu (to 1am Fri & Sat), 11:30am–10pm Sun

Located on Norr Mälarstrand, this is a café by day and bar at night.

Bar at BrewDog Kungsholmen

Places to Eat

PRICE CATEGORIES
For a three-course meal for one with half a bottle of wine (or equivalent meal), taxes and extra charges.

Kr under 700 kr KrKr 700–1,000 kr
KrKrKr over 1,000 kr

1 Linguini

MAP B1 ■ Frejgatan 48 ■ 08 31 49 15 ■ Open 5–9pm Mon–Thu (to 11:30pm Fri & Sat) ■ Kr

With a cosy setting, Linguini serves good Italian food. Book in advance, as there are only around 10 tables.

2 Clas på Hörnet

MAP C1 ■ Surbrunnsgatan 20 ■ 08 16 51 36 ■ Open 5pm–midnight Sat & Mon, 11:30am–midnight Tue–Fri ■ Kr

Housed in an 18th-century building, this hotel serves Swedish dishes, all made with fresh, organic ingredients.

3 Svartengrens

MAP C1 ■ Tulegatan 24 ■ 08 612 65 50 ■ Open 5pm–11pm Wed–Sun (to 1am Fri & Sat) ■ KrKrKr

This restaurant serves ecologically sourced food and good cocktails.

4 Wasahof

MAP B2 ■ Dalagatan 46 ■ 08 32 34 40 ■ Open 4pm–midnight Mon–Tue (to 1pm Wed–Sat) ■ KrKr

This classic French bistro is famed for its seafood. Oysters are a specialty.

5 Spisa Hos Helena

MAP B3 ■ Scheelegatan 18 ■ 08 654 49 26 ■ Open 11am–midnight Mon–Fri, 4pm–midnight Sat (to 11pm Sun) ■ Kr

The Sunday set menu offers great value at this cosy and popular bistro.

6 Tennstopet

MAP B2 ■ Dalagatan 50 ■ 08 32 25 18 ■ Open 11:30am–1am Mon–Fri, 1pm–1am Sat–Sun ■ KrKrKr

Relive the 1940s and 1950s in this place serving classic Swedish food.

7 Lux Dag för Dag

Primusgatan 116 ■ 08 619 01 90 ■ Open 11:30am–2pm & 5–11pm Tue–Fri, 5–11pm Sat ■ Kr

This bistro-restaurant offers seasonal cooking with locally sourced fresh produce.

Chic interior of Lux Dag för Dag

8 Stadshuskällaren

MAP C4 ■ Hantverkargatan 1 ■ 08 586 218 30 ■ Open 11:30am–2:30pm Mon–Tue, 11:30am–2:30pm & 5–11pm Wed–Fri, 5–11pm Sat ■ KrKrKr

Sample Nobel Prize banquet menus served since 1901 in the atmospheric vaulted cellar of Stadshuset.

9 Trattorian

MAP B4 ■ Norr Mälarstrand 9, Kajplats 464 ■ 08 684 238 70 ■ Open 5–11pm Mon–Thu (to midnight Fri), 11:30am–2:30pm & 5pm–midnight Sat, 11:30am–6pm Sun ■ KrKr

Classic Italian cuisine is served on a waterside pontoon, with fabulous views across the water at sunset.

10 Lilla Ego

MAP B1 ■ Västmannagatan 69 ■ 08 27 44 55 ■ Open 5–11pm Tue–Sat ■ KrKrKr

Enjoy robust, seasonal dishes prepared by award-winning chefs here *(see p54)*. Book well in advance.

See map on p70 ←

TOP 10 Östermalm and Djurgården

Although these two districts are neighbours, Östermalm and Djurgården offer contrasting experiences. Östermalm is Stockholm's most exclusive address, home to palatial residences and some of the city's most expensive restaurants and designer shops. Djurgården, on a separate island across the water, is a green oasis, home to only 800 permanent residents and part of the Stockholm National City Park. Most of its eastern end is undisturbed parkland with excellent walks, while the western part has some of Stockholm's top attractions – Skansen, Junibacken, Vasamuseet and Gröna Lund funfair are all found here.

Carl Linnaeus statue, Humlegården

ÖSTERMALM AND DJURGÅRDEN

0 metres 500
0 yards 500

RUNEBERGS-PLAN
FLORAG
STURE G.
BRAHEGATAN
TURE GATAN
ÖSTERMALMSGATAN
VALHALLA-VÄGEN
KARLAVÄGEN
Stadion
Humlegården
ERIK DAHLBERGSALLÉN
VARTAVÄGEN
Karlaplan
KARLAPLAN
KOMMENDÖRSGATAN
STURE GATAN
BRAHEGATAN
GREV
LINNEGATAN
JUNGFRUG.
ARTILLERIGATAN
SKEPPARGATAN
BANÉRGATAN
Gustav Adolfsparken
ENGELBREKTS-PLAN
BRUNNSG.
KUNGSG.
NORRLANDSG.
HUMLEGÅRDSGATAN
Östermalmstorg
ÖSTERMALM
KARLAVÄGEN
GYLLENSTIERNSG.
OXENSTIERNSGATAN
MÄSTER SAMUELSGATAN
NORR-MALMSTORG
NYBROGATAN
SIBYLLEGATAN
ARTILLERIGATAN
SKEPPARG.
RIDDARG.
GREVGATAN
STYRMANSG.
NARVAVÄGEN
STORGATAN
BANÉG.
LINNEGATAN
ULRIKAGATAN
GÄRDESG.
STRANDVÄGEN
Diplomatstaden
Nobel-parken
KRUTHUS-PLAN
REGERINGS-GATAN
Kungsträdgården
Berzeli Park
Nybroplan
STRANDVÄGEN
Djurgårdsbron
Kungsträdgården
KARL XII:S TORG
GUSTAV ADOLFS TORG
NYBROKAJEN
STALLGATAN
Ladugårdslands-viken
Nybroviken
Galärparken
Djurgårdsbrunnsviken
BLASIE-HOLMEN
STRÖMKAJEN
Strömbron
RIKS-PLAN
SLOTTSKAJEN
Norrström
Skeppsholmsbron
Djurgården
SÖDRA VARVSPORTEN
ROSENDALSVÄGEN
1 km (0.6 miles)
DJURGÅRDSVÄGEN
HAZELIUSBACKEN
SKEPPSHOLMEN
SVENSKSUNDS VÄGEN
Skepps-holmen
FALKENBERGSGATAN
ÅNGAG.
DJURGÅRDEN
SÖLLIDSBACKEN
Allmänna gränd
Kastellholmsbron
Kastell-parken
Kastellholmen
Beckholmssundet
Djurgårds-staden

1 Top 10 Sights *see pp77–9*
1 Places to Eat *see p81*
1 Cafés, Bars and Pubs *see p80*

1 Humlegården

MAP M1

Just a stone's throw away from Stureplan, the broad, oak tree-lined paths and lawns of Humlegården *(see p45)*, or "Hop Garden", are a welcome retreat from the busy city centre. This former royal garden has been a public park since 1869, and has a large play area and, in the summer, outdoor clubs and bars. A statue of Swedish naturalist Carl Linnaeus looks out over the middle of the park. Humlegården is also home to the National Library of Sweden.

2 Historiska Museet

The Swedish History Museum *(see pp32–3)* is a showcase for collections from Prehistory through the Viking era to the Middle Ages. Fantastic artifacts include ancient gold jewellery, while a reconstruction shows what a small rural church in Västergötland looked like at the end of the Middle Ages. Discover how people lived, worked and ate during the prehistoric times and view priceless archaeological finds that were discovered after 3,000 years. The Viking exhibitions reveal how these people were often peaceful traders rather than brutal robbers.

3 Walk along Djurgårdsbrunnsviken

MAP R4

Alight from the bus or tram at Djurgårdsbron, opposite Nordiska Museet. Walk through the bright blue gates to pick up the path along Rosendalsvägen, by the water's edge, and watch gleaming mahogany boats, canoes and pedalos glide past. The path leads towards the biodynamic market garden and café at Rosendals Trädgård *(see p80)*.

Bridge across Djurgårdsbrunnsviken

4 Gröna Lund

By the Djurgården waterfront, Gröna Lund *(see pp28–9)* is both an amusement park and a major concert venue. The funfair features over 30 attractions, including seven roller coasters and one of the world's highest free fall towers. The Eclipse ride is the world's highest StarFlyer at 122m (400 ft). The park also includes vintage carousels and side-shows. There are numerous restaurants, bars and fast food outlets.

Gröna Lund amusement park

Exhibition hall, Nordiska Museet

5 Nordiska Museet

This lovely museum *(see pp30–31)* charts everyday life in Sweden from the 16th century to the present day via a huge number of exhibits. The exhibitions focus on periods of major change and transition – fashion trends are explored from the 1780s, 1860s and 1960s, while a section dedicated to interiors covers both the elaborate styles of the 19th century as well as the practical considerations made for the country's housing boom of the 1970s. Visitors can also find out about how local Swedish traditions such as dancing around the maypole to celebrate Midsummer originated.

6 Skansen

Located in a beautiful hilly spot on Djurgården, Skansen *(see pp12–13)* is deservedly one of the city's most enduring attractions. Journey through Sweden over the ages, taking in examples of historic houses and farmsteads from every era and part of the country. Interactive exhibits and costumed staff transport you back in time, demonstrating crafts such as glass blowing, bookbinding and baking. Many activities are family-focussed, particularly the model school and gentle fairground rides.

7 ABBA The Museum

MAP R5 ■ Djurgårdsvägen 68 ■ 08 121 328 60 ■ Opening hours vary, check website for details ■ Adm ■ www.abbathemuseum.com

Fans of the Swedish pop sensation ABBA will love this museum *(see p42)*, which features a multitude of interactive displays. Visitors can put on the legendary stage costumes and sing alongside hologram illusions of the band at Polar Studio. The Folkpark exhibition transports visitors to 1966, when the ABBA phenomenon started, as this was where Benny and Björn first met. In addition, listen to the band members' own stories and memories from their amazing award-winning careers.

8 Vasamuseet

Getting up close to the *Vasa*, the best-preserved 17th-century warship in the world, is a unique and memorable experience. Built as the jewel of the Swedish fleet, she sank just minutes into her maiden voyage from Stockholm in 1628, and lay undisturbed for 333 years. In 1961, an extraordinary salvage operation raised the ship – different exhibitions inside the Vasamuseet *(see pp14–15)* describe the story of the vessel and its impressive restoration.

Bünsowska Huset, Strandvägen

ÖSTERMALM'S ARCHITECTURE

Östermalm was developed in the late 19th century around the four tree-lined boulevards of Karlavägen, Strandvägen, Valhallavägen and Narvavägen. Some of Sweden's best architects of the era, such as Gustaf Dahl who designed the Kungliga Biblioteke and Isak Gustaf Clason who created Bünsowska Huset on Strandvägen, shaped the district in a Renaissance style.

9 Stureplan
MAP M2

Originally just the name of a square with a quirky mushroom-shaped rain shelter at its heart, "Stureplan" has become synonymous with luxury and style. On the streets radiating from it are exclusive fashion houses, costly restaurants, bars and clubs.

10 Strandvägen
MAP P3

Completed in time for Stockholm's World Fair in 1897, Strandvägen is one of the most prestigious streets in the city. Running almost parallel to the waterside of Nybroviken, the wide boulevard has an air of old grandeur, enhanced by the vintage trams that rattle along it. Bünsowska Huset, at Nos 29–33, designed by local architects Isak Gustaf Clason and Anders Gustaf Forsberg, sets the standard for the street. The tree-lined middle of the street shades the walking and cycling lanes, while wooden ships line the quays.

A DAY IN ÖSTERMALM AND DJURGÅRDEN

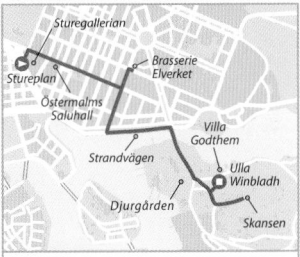

MORNING

Start off, like thousands of people do, at the concrete "mushroom" meeting spot right on **Stureplan**. Directly behind the sculpture is Sturegallerian (Stureplan 4), an ideal place to shop for exclusive brands or browse the Hedengrens bookshop, which stocks books in many languages. There are also several cafés to choose from for an energizing morning coffee – the cosy Konditoriet is recommended. Next, head for the shopping heart of Östermalm in the streets surrounding Östermalmstorg. Drop by the **Östermalms Saluhall**, a 19th-century food hall located on the square, to stock up on some Swedish delicacies. From there, it is a short walk to **Brasserie Elverket** *(see p81)*, on Linnégatan, which is an excellent choice for lunch on weekdays with several good-value dishes of the day.

AFTERNOON

Burn off the calories after lunch by strolling down to **Strandvägen**; either continue along the lovely waterside boulevard admiring the architecture, or hop on to a bus or tram to the parkland island of **Djurgården** *(see p45)*. Alight at **Skansen** *(see pp12–13)* and set aside an afternoon to wander around its old town and rustic farmhouses. Round off the day with a classic Swedish dinner at **Ulla Windbladh** *(see p81)*. If that is fully booked, the nearby **Villa Godthem** *(see p81)* is a good second option; both have outdoor seating in summer.

See map on p76

Cafés, Bars and Pubs

1 Rosendals Trädgård

MAP G4 ■ Rosendalsterrassen 12 ■ 08 545 812 70 ■ Open Apr–Sep: 11am–5pm daily; Oct–Mar: 11am–4pm daily; closed Jan ■ www.rosendalstradgard.se

A garden café *(see p53)* in Djurgården sells homemade organic salads, soups, sandwiches and pastries.

2 Blå Porten

MAP R5 ■ Djurgårdsvägen 64 ■ 08 663 87 59 ■ Open 11am–9pm Tue–Thu, 11am–7pm Fri–Mon

Close to Gröna Lund, Skansen and Vasamuseet, Blå Porten offers a wide-ranging self-service menu.

Riche, a classic Stockholm bar

3 Riche

MAP N2 ■ Birger Jarlsgatan 4 ■ 08 545 035 60 ■ Open 7:30am–midnight Mon (to 1am Tue, to 2am Wed–Fri), 11am–2am Sat, noon–midnight Sun

A meeting place with several bars.

4 Sturekatten

MAP N2 ■ Riddargatan 4 ■ 08 611 16 12 ■ Open 9am–7pm Mon–Fri (to 6pm Sat), 10am–6pm Sun

The "Sture Cat" is an old-fashioned tea and coffee house *(see p52)* in an apartment building from the 1700s.

5 East

MAP M2 ■ Stureplan 13 ■ 08 611 49 59 ■ Open 11:30am–3am Mon–Fri, noon–3am Sat & Sun

East serves Asian food by day, and turns into a nightclub after 11pm.

6 Obaren Sturehof

MAP M2 ■ Sturegallerian 42, Stureplan 2 ■ 08 440 57 30 ■ Open 11am–2am Mon–Sat, noon–2am Sun

Central to Stureplan's busy club scene, Obaren is a good choice for those who just want to party.

7 Scandic Anglais

MAP D2 ■ Humlegårdsgatan 23 ■ 08 517 340 00 ■ Open 9am–midnight Mon–Tue (to 2am Wed–Sat), 11am–midnight Sun

With three bars and a summer rooftop terrace, Scandic Anglais has DJs most nights and attracts an after-work and late-night party crowd.

8 Valhallabageriet

MAP R1 ■ Valhallavägen 174 ■ 08 662 97 63 ■ Open 7am–6pm Mon–Fri, 8am–3pm Sat, 9am–3pm Sun

New sourdough bakeries seem to spring up every week in Stockholm, but Valhallabageriet is an enduring favourite. It also serves coffee and fabulous Swedish buns and pastries.

9 Saturnus

MAP D2 ■ Eriksbergsgatan 6 ■ 08 611 77 00 ■ Open 7am–8pm Mon–Fri, 8am–7pm Sat & Sun

This Parisian-style café *(see p52)* and lunch spot serves big bowls of coffee with cinnamon buns to match. It also serves breakfast and brunch and offers its customers a selection of international newspapers to read.

10 Tudor Arms

MAP P2 ■ Grevgatan 31 ■ 08 660 27 12 ■ Open 4–11pm Mon, 11am–11pm Tue–Fri, 1–11pm Sat (to 7pm Sun)

British pub the Tudor Arms has been open since 1969.

See map on p76

Places to Eat

PRICE CATEGORIES

For a three-course meal for one with half a bottle of wine (or equivalent meal), taxes and extra charges.

Ⓚ under 700 kr ⓀⓀ 700–1,000 kr ⓀⓀⓀ over 1,000 kr

1 Villa Godthem

MAP R4 ■ Rosendalsvägen 9 ■ 08 684 238 40 ■ Open 11:30am–10pm Mon–Thu (to 11pm Fri), noon–11pm Sat (to 9:30pm Sun) ■ Ⓚ

Located in a 19th-century wooden house set deep in Djugården parkland, Villa Godthem serves classic gourmet Swedish dishes.

2 Sturehof

MAP M2 ■ Stureplan 2 ■ 08 440 57 30 ■ Open 11am–2am Mon–Sat, noon–2am Sun ■ ⓀⓀ

With a history that spans over a century, this classic restaurant *(see p55)* specializes in seafood.

3 Ekstedt

MAP D2 ■ Humlegårdsgatan 17 ■ 08 611 12 10 ■ Open 6pm–1am Tue–Thu, 5pm–1am Fri, 4pm–1am Sat ■ ⓀⓀⓀ

Rustic four- or six-course set menus are cooked on an open, wood fire at chef Niklas Ekstedt's signature Stockholm restaurant *(see p55)*.

4 Teatergrillen

MAP N2 ■ Nybrogatan 3 ■ 08 545 035 65 ■ Open 11:30am–10pm Mon & Tue (to midnight Wed & Thu, to 1am Fri), noon–1am Sat ■ ⓀⓀⓀ

This place is an excellent French-Swedish crossover restaurant.

5 Brasserie Elverket

MAP Q2 ■ Linnégatan 69 ■ 08 661 25 62 ■ Open L: 11am–2pm Mon–Fri; D: 5–9pm Mon–Thu (to 10pm Fri) ■ Ⓚ

The lunches at this French-inspired brasserie are superb value and it serves craft beers on tap.

6 Gastrologik

MAP D3 ■ Artillerigatan 14 ■ 08 662 30 60 ■ Open 6–11:30pm Tue–Sat ■ ⓀⓀⓀ

Experience new Nordic cuisine here *(see p54)*. The tasting menu is updated daily to feature fresh local produce.

7 Grodan

MAP N2 ■ Grev Turegatan 16 ■ 08 679 61 00 ■ Open 7:30am–11pm Mon (to midnight Tue–Thu, to 1am Fri), noon–1am Sat (to 10pm Sun) ■ ⓀⓀ

A classic Swedish-European fusion restaurant with an adjacent bar.

8 PA & Co

MAP N2 ■ Riddargatan 8 ■ 08 611 08 45 ■ Open 5pm–midnight daily ■ Ⓚ

Swedish food with a twist is served in an intimate space.

9 Cassi

MAP Q2 ■ Narvavägen 30 ■ 08 661 74 61 ■ Open 10:45am–8pm Mon–Fri, 1–8pm Sun ■ ⓀⓀ

Go back to the 1970s in this popular family-run French bistro.

10 Ulla Winbladh

MAP R4 ■ Rosendalsvägen 8 ■ 08 534 897 01 ■ Open 11:30am–10pm Mon, 11:30am–11pm Tue–Fri (to 10pm Sun), 12:30–11pm Sat ■ ⓀⓀ

This traditional, historic Swedish inn is located close to Djurgårdsbron.

Alfresco dining at Ulla Winbladh

TOP 10 Gamla Stan, Skeppsholmen and Blasieholmen

Lion statue by the Royal Palace

The site of Stockholm's 13th-century origins and a well-preserved medieval city centre, Gamla Stan (Old Town) is one of Stockholm's most popular destinations. Away from tourist crowds, however, the narrow streets have a fairy-tale like feel, particularly at night and when it is snowing. The vast and rather sombre-looking Royal Palace is the major attraction, and there are also many beautiful churches, including Storkyrkan. Skeppsholmen is famous for its excellent museums – Moderna Museet, with its collection of 20th-century art, and Östasiatiska Museet, housing Far Eastern antiquities, are two of them. The luxurious Grand Hotel dominates neighbouring Blasieholmen, which is also home to the Nationalmuseum.

GAMLA STAN, SKEPPSHOLMEN AND BLASIEHOLMEN

Central Gamla Stan
KLEJMENS GRÅGRÅ
JGNATIIGRÅND GÅSGRÅND
ANKARGR.
STORKYRKANS GÅRD
TRÄNGSUND
SPEKTENS GRÅND
SOLGRÅND
STORTORGET
D. FICKS GR.
VÄSTERLÅNGGATAN
PRÄSTGATAN
SKOMAKARGATAN
YXSMEDS GRÅND
STORA NYGATAN
BRÖDERS GRÅND
SKOMAKARGRÅND
LILLA NYGATAN
VÄRBINKEN
TYSKA BRINKEN
0 metres 70
0 yards 70

KUNGSTRÄDGÅRDSG.
BLASIEHOLMS TORG
NYBROMAJEN
STALLGATAN
BLASIEHOLMSTEATERG.
HOVSLÅGARGATAN
STRÖMKAJEN
BLASIE-HOLMEN
KARL XII:S TORG
Norrbro
Strömbron
Helgeandsholmen
RIKSPLAN
MUSEIKAJEN
Norrström
Stallgränden
SLOTTSKAJEN
Skeppsholmsbron
Stallbron
Vasabron
MYNTGATA
MYNT-TORGET
SLOTTSBACKEN
RIDDARHUS-TORGET
STORKYRKO BRINKEN
See inset above
BIRGER JARLS TORG
Riddarholmen
KÖPMANG.
KÖPMAN-TORGET
KÖPMANG.
Strömmen
VÄSTERLÅNGGATAN
STORA NYGATAN
LILLA
SVARTMANG
VINDSTUG.
SJÖLAGÅRDSG.
ÖSTERLÅNGG.
SKEPPSBRON
SKEPPSBROKAJEN
CENTRALBRON
MUNKBROG.
NYGATAN
TYSKA BRINKEN
GAMLA STAN
Gamla Stan
KORNHAMNS-TORG
SÖDRA BANKOGRÄND
Söderström
SLUSSPLAN
Slussen
Area under redevelopment
KARL JOHANS TORG
0 metres 200
0 yards 200

Previous pages *Södermalm waterfront*

The small island of Riddarholmen, dominated by Riddarholmskyrkan

1 Riddarholmen

MAP L5 ■ Birger Jarls Torg ■ www.kungahuset.se

The "Knight's Island" is cut off from Gamla Stan by a major road and a river, but is worth the diversion. The island has some of the best views from Evert Taubes Terrass across the water to Lake Mälaren. Riddarholmen is home to Riddarholmskyrkan *(see p40)* and many 17th-century palaces, which now house offices. Walpurgis Night *(see p61)* is celebrated here with a bonfire and singing.

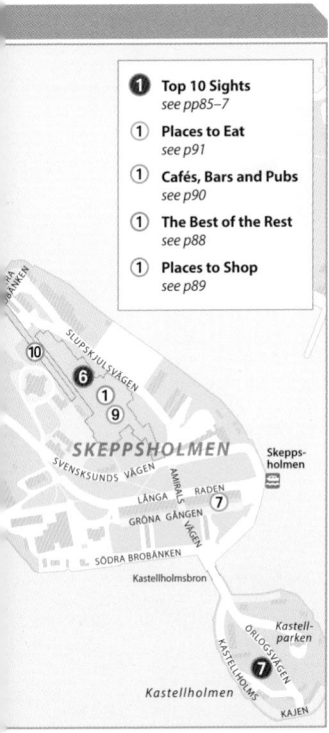

2 Nationalmuseum

MAP N4 ■ www.nationalmuseum.se

This museum *(see p43)* houses Sweden's largest art collection, with some 16,000 paintings and sculptures. There is a huge collection of artifacts from the Renaissance to the present. The museum also hosts temporary exhibitions.

3 The Royal Palace (Kungliga Slottet)

With more than 600 rooms, the Royal Palace *(see pp26–7)* is one of the biggest in Europe and still the venue for all state functions. It houses five museums, including the Treasury, in the cellar vaults, with priceless state regalia such as crowns.

Gustav III's bedroom, the Royal Palace

4 Storkyrkan

MAP M5 ■ Trångsund 1 ■ www.svenskakyrkan.se/stockholmsdomkyrkoforsamling

Stockholm's medieval cathedral *(see p40)*, built in the 14th century, is of great religious importance. It is renowned for its art treasures, including *St George and the Dragon* (1489), a sculpture carved from oak and elk horn. The legendary *Vädersolstavlan*, the "Sun Dog Painting", from 1535, is the oldest portrayal of the capital painted from high up on the cliffs of Södermalm. A wide range of services and concerts are held here.

The red-brick nave of Storkyrkan

5 Stortorget

MAP M5

A small public square, Stortorget, in the middle of Gamla Stan, is the oldest square in Stockholm and the site of the "Stockholm Bloodbath" in 1520 *(see p38)*. Unlike many other European city squares, it was never developed as a showpiece: it has a distinct westward slope, and its buildings were constructed in a haphazard manner in the 17th and 18th centuries. The Stock Exchange Building (Börshuset), in French Rococo style, was completed in 1776 and houses the Nobelmuseet *(see p88)*. In a second-hand shop on Stortorget 5, there are ceiling joists dating from the 1640s with pictures of animals, flowers and fruits.

SLUSSEN REDEVELOPMENT

One of the most historically important junctions in Stockholm is undergoing a controversial transformation. The area around Slussen – the lock between the Baltic and Lake Mälaren, joining Gamla Stan and Södermalm – is being rebuilt to improve traffic flow and to create a new park, plaza and buildings. Building work is expected to last until 2030.

6 Moderna Museet

MAP P4 ■ Exercisplan 4 ■ 08 520 235 00 ■ Open 10am–8pm Tue, 10am–6pm Wed–Sun ■ www.modernamuseet.se

Set on the leafy Skeppsholmen island, this museum exhibits key works of 20th-century art, including those by Dalí, Picasso, Matisse, Giorgio de Chirico and many more. The collection includes some 6,000 paintings, sculptures and installations, as well as drawings and photography. The museum also hosts exhibitions of contemporary Swedish and international art. There is a children's workshop, a shop and a restaurant with views across the water to Djurgården and Strandvägen *(see pp42–3)*.

7 Kastellholmen

MAP Q6

South of Skeppsholmen is the tiny island of Kastellholmen, part of the national city park. Take a picnic, find a comfortable spot on its granite rocks, watch the boats go by and admire the Kastellet, the island's castle-like medieval building.

Kastellet on Kastellholmen

The *af Chapman* on Skeppsholmen

8 Skeppsholmen Shoreline Walk

MAP P4

Skeppsholmen is ideal for a circular waterside walk any time of the year. Cross Skeppsholmsbron to the island, turn left and follow the path through a small doorway, and along the water to the quayside Östra Brobänken. Take in the veteran boats moored here, and the views across the water. Catch a Djurgården ferry at the southeastern tip of the island, or continue past the three-mast *af Chapman (see p117)*, now a hostel.

9 Christmas Market

MAP M5 ■ Stortorget ■ 4th Sat in Nov–23 Dec: 11am–6pm daily

The magical atmosphere of the Stockholm winter is most evident at the traditional Christmas market in Stortorget. Little red huts sell home-made products – Christmas lights and decorations, handicrafts, festive sweets, smoked sausages, reindeer and elk meat and other delicacies from around Sweden. Get warm with a glass or two of *glögg* (mulled wine).

10 Streets of Gamla Stan

MAP M5

Västerlånggatan is the Old Town's main street, and, although busy, it is no longer as touristy as it used to be. At its southern end is Mårten Trotzigs Gränd, the city's narrowest street. More relaxed Österlånggatan is home to several restaurants and unique shops, and the charming Köpmangatan is a good street to unwind, with its cafés and bars.

A DAY IN GAMLA STAN, SKEPPSHOLMEN & BLASIEHOLMEN

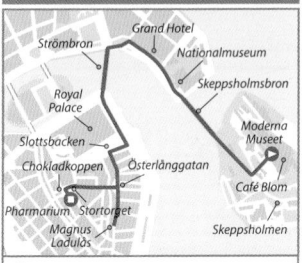

MORNING

Start the day with a visit to two of Stockholm's best museums: bus 65 from Stockholm's Central Station runs all the way to the island of **Skeppsholmen**. Here, head for the **Moderna Museet**. After a good morning's viewing of its fine 20th-century art collection, take a coffee break at **Café Blom** *(see p90)*, located within the museum. Walk over Skeppsholmsbron towards Blasieholmen and head past the ferries to the **Nationalmuseum** *(see p85)* and the **Grand Hotel** *(see p113)* before swinging back across Strömbron towards the **Royal Palace** *(see p85)*. Walk up the cobbled Slottsbacken, and on to Gamla Stan's Österlånggatan. A good lunch stop here is **Magnus Ladulås** *(see p91)*; enjoy a three-course meal in their traditional cellar restaurant.

AFTERNOON

Get purposefully lost along the narrow yet charming streets around Köpmangatan, aiming to end up at **Stortorget**, the Old Town's magnificent main square. Admire the square with a hot chocolate at **Chokladkoppen** *(see p90)*. The afternoon can be one of the least busy times on Västerlånggatan; stroll southeast along it and drop into the best of its shops for a leisurely browse. At the eastern end, do not miss the Old Town's narrowest street, Mårten Trotzigs Gränd. Round off the day with a drink and some snacks with the locals at the popular **Pharmarium** *(see p90)*.

See map on pp84–5 ←

The Best of the Rest

Models showing changes in historical architectural styles, ArkDes

1 ArkDes

MAP P5 ■ Exercisplan 4, Skeppsholmen ■ 08 587 270 00 ■ Open 10am–8pm Tue & Fri (to 6pm Wed & Thu), 11am–6pm Sat & Sun ■ Adm ■ www.arkdes.se

Explore Swedish architecture from 1,000 years ago to the present day.

2 Evert Taubes Terrass

MAP L5 ■ Riddarholmen

A statue of Evert Taube (1890–1976), troubadour and ballad writer, stands on the terrace below Wrangelska Palatset overlooking Riddarfjärden.

3 Tyska Kyrkan

MAP M5 ■ Svartmangatan 16 ■ 08 411 11 88 ■ Open Jun–Aug: 10:30am–4:30pm daily; Sep–May: 11am–3pm Fri & Sat, 12:30–4pm Sun ■ Adm ■ www.svenskakyrkan.se/deutschegemeinde

This church was founded in 1571.

4 Story Tours

MAP M5 ■ 070 490 62 69 ■ Adm ■ www.storytours.eu

Discover the Old Town's charms on a walking tour around Gamla Stan.

5 Nobelmuseet

MAP M5 ■ Stortorget ■ 08 534 818 00 ■ Open Jun–Aug: 10am–8pm daily; mid-Sep–May: 11am–8pm Tue (to 5pm Wed–Sun) ■ Adm ■ www.nobelprizemuseum.se

Learn all about the history of the Nobel Prize and its winners.

6 Livrustkammaren

MAP M5 ■ Slottsbacken 3 ■ 08 402 30 30 ■ Open 11am–5pm daily (to 8pm Thu) ■ Adm ■ www.livrustkammaren.se

The Royal Armoury has a collection of objects from Swedish royalty.

7 Forum För Levande Historia

MAP M5 ■ Stora Nygatan 10 ■ 08 723 87 50 ■ Open noon–5pm Mon–Fri ■ www.levandehistoria.se

The Forum for Living History promotes tolerance and human rights.

8 Postmuseum

MAP M5 ■ Lilla Nygatan 6 ■ 01 043 644 39 ■ Open 11am–4pm Tue–Sun (Sep–Apr: to 7pm Wed) ■ Adm ■ www.postmuseum.posten.se

This museum traces the history of the Swedish postal system.

9 Jarnpojke

MAP E4 ■ Bollhustäppan

Located just left of the Finska Kyrkan, this 15-cm (5.9-in) statue depicts a boy looking at the moon. Leaving a gift for the statue is said to bring good luck.

10 Östasiatiska Museet

MAP P4 ■ Tyghusplan, Skeppsholmen ■ 08 519 557 50 ■ Open 11am–8pm Tue (to 5pm Wed–Sun) ■ Adm ■ www.ostasiatiska.se

This museum has superb collections from the Far East and Asia.

Places to Shop

1 Gudrun Sjödén

MAP M5 ■ Stora Nygatan 33 ■ 08 23 55 55 ■ www.gudrunsjoden.com

This place sells colourful clothes for women with an emphasis on Scandinavian style. The garments have been designed by Gudrun Sjödén herself since the 1970s.

2 Iris Hantverk

MAP M5 ■ Västerlånggatan 24 ■ 08 698 09 73

This 19th-century shop sells beautifully designed brushes made by visually impaired craftspeople.

3 Earth N More

MAP M5 ■ Stora Nygatan 14 ■ 08 641 02 10 ■ Open 11am–6pm Mon–Fri (to 4pm Sat) ■ www.earthnmore.com

This environmentally conscious store sells clothes and accessories that "combine design, function and environment in an attractive way".

Floral dresses, Earth N More

4 Blå Gungan

MAP M5 ■ Österlånggatan 16 ■ 08 20 23 73 ■ Open 11am–6pm Mon–Fri (to 4pm Sat) ■ www.blagungan.se

Quirky interior design pieces, accessories, garments and more by mainly Swedish designers.

5 Hilda Hilda

MAP M5 ■ Österlånggatan 21 ■ 08 641 36 80

Founded in 1995, this shop offers home decor and accessories made out of ecological yarn, woven in Sweden with their Indigenous weaving method.

6 Happy Sthlm

MAP M5 ■ Västerlånggatan 40 & 68 ■ Open 11am–6pm daily ■ www.stutterheim.com

Building on Sweden's long heritage of crafting weatherproof gear, designer Alexander Stutterheim has proven that raincoats can not only be practical but also fashionable. His colourful jackets and accessories, are all handmade in Sweden.

7 Krabat

MAP M5 ■ Stora Nygatan 21 ■ 08 21 49 24 ■ Open 10am–6pm Mon–Fri (to 4pm Sat), 11am–4pm Sun ■ www.krabat.se

The classic and durable toys in the shop's own design are sold next to international brands. Items range from dolls and cars to costumes.

8 SF Bokhandeln

MAP M5 ■ Västerlånggatan 48 ■ 08 21 50 52

A haven for lovers of science fiction, this store sells books, films, games and magazines. A large amount of its stock is in English.

9 Edblad

MAP M5 ■ Västerlånggatan 36 ■ 08 519 90 092 ■ Open 10am–6pm Mon–Fri (to 5pm Sat), 11am–4pm Sun ■ www.edblad.com

Designers Hans and Cathrine Edblad create beautiful jewellery, clothing and home furnishings made with sustainability in mind. Everything is made in their studio on Singö island.

10 Made In Stockholm

MAP M5 ■ Västerlånggatan 58 ■ 08 411 46 07 ■ Open 11am–6pm Mon–Fri (to 4pm Sat & Sun) ■ www.madeinstockholm.nu

Glassware, ceramics, silverware and other handcrafted items are stocked here, made by local artisans.

See map on pp84–5 ←

Cafés, Bars and Pubs

1 Corner Club

MAP D4 ■ Lilla Nygatan 16 ■ 08 20 85 83 ■ Open 5pm–midnight Wed–Sat

A local favourite, Corner Club offers an extensive cocktail list. If you get hungry, head downstairs to the sister gastropub, The Flying Elk.

2 Wirströms Pub

MAP M5 ■ Stora Nygatan 13 ■ 08 21 28 74 ■ Open 2pm–1am Tue–Thu (to midnight Mon), noon–1am Fri & Sun, 11am–1am Sat

This popular pub attracts a mix of students, tourists and locals.

3 Stampen

MAP M5 ■ Stora Nygatan 5 ■ 08 20 57 93 ■ Open 5pm–1am Tue–Fri, 2pm–1am Sat, 5pm–1am Sun

Founded in 1968, this long-standing jazz and blues bar has live music.

4 Ardbeg Embassy

MAP M5 ■ Västerlånggatan 68 ■ 08 791 90 90 ■ Opening times vary, call ahead

A whisky bar with a wide selection of beers from Swedish micro-breweries. It serves high-quality, pricey food, too.

5 Pharmarium

MAP M5 ■ Stortorget 7 ■ 08 20 08 10 ■ Open 4:30–11pm Mon, Tue & Sun (to midnight Wed & Thu, to 1am Fri & Sat)

Housed in Sweden's first pharmacy, this cocktail bar serves signature drinks paired with snacks.

6 Lydmar Hotel Bar

MAP N4 ■ Södra Blasieholmshamnen 2 ■ 08 22 31 60 ■ Open 11am–1am daily

Great drinks are served in this stylish bar located in the Lydmar Hotel. In summer relax on the rooftop patio.

7 Caffellini

MAP M5 ■ Västerlånggatan 67 ■ 070 676 60 16 ■ Open 8am–4pm Mon–Fri, 10am–6pm Sat

Enjoy great espresso in this small café.

8 Chokladkoppen

MAP M5 ■ Stortorget 18 ■ 08 20 31 70 ■ Summer: open 9am–11pm daily; winter: open 10am–10pm Mon–Thu, 10am–11pm Fri, 9am–11pm Sat, 9am–10pm Sun

A LGBTQ+-friendly café *(see p53)* in the Old Town's main square. Try the delicious hot chocolate here.

9 Café Blom

MAP P4 ■ Exercisplan 4, Skeppsholmen ■ 08 527 546 50 ■ Open 11am–7:30pm Tue & Fri, 11am–5:30pm Wed, Thu, Sat & Sun

Located close to Moderna Museet and ArkDes, this café serves snacks and pastries. It also has a covered outdoor area in Picasso Park.

10 Cadier Bar, Grand Hotel

MAP N4 ■ Södra Blaiseholmshamnen 8 ■ 08 679 35 85 ■ Open 7am–2am Mon–Fri, 8am–2am Sat, 8am–1am Sun

Enjoy delicious breakfast, brunch, an afternoon tea or a cocktail at Grand Hotel's elegant bar.

Swanky Cadier Bar in the Grand Hotel

Places to Eat

PRICE CATEGORIES

For a three-course meal for one with half a bottle of wine (or equivalent meal), taxes and extra charges.

Ⓚ under 700 kr ⓀⓀ 700–1,000 kr ⓀⓀⓀ over 1,000 kr

1 Tradition

MAP N5 ■ Österlånggatan 1 ■ 08 20 35 25 ■ Open 11:30am–11pm Mon–Fri, 4–11pm Sat (to 10pm Sun) ■ ⓀⓀ

Experience traditional home-cooked Swedish cuisine at this restaurant.

2 Matbaren

MAP N4 ■ Södra Blaiseholmshamnen 6 ■ 08 679 35 84 ■ Open noon–2pm & 6pm–midnight Mon–Fri ■ ⓀⓀ

Enjoy fresh seasonal produce at this Michelin-starred bistro *(see p54)*.

3 B.A.R.

MAP N3 ■ Blasieholmsgatan 4a ■ 08 611 53 35 ■ Open 5–10pm Tue–Sat ■ ⓀⓀ

Excellent seafood restaurant; pick from grilled fish of the day.

4 The Flying Elk

MAP D4 ■ Mälartorget 15 ■ 08 20 85 83 ■ Open 5pm–midnight Mon–Thu (to 1am Fri & Sat), 4–11pm Sun ■ ⓀⓀ

Swedish culinary tradition meets British pub culture at Swede Björn Frantzén's gastropub *(see p52)*.

5 Bistro Pastis

MAP M5 ■ Baggensgatan 12 ■ 08 20 20 18 ■ Open 4–10pm Mon–Wed, 11:30am– 3:30pm & 5–11pm Thu & Fri, noon–11pm Sat & Sun ■ ⓀⓀ

A French bistro with a homely, modern feel, serving delicious Gallic cuisine.

6 Djuret

MAP M5 ■ Lilla Nygatan 5 ■ 08 506 400 84 ■ Open 5:30pm–midnight Tue–Sat ■ ⓀⓀ

With its name meaning "The Animal", Djuret is a meat-eater's paradise.

7 Långa Raden

MAP P5 ■ Gröna Gången 1 ■ 08 407 23 05 ■ Open 11:30am–9pm Mon–Fri, noon–9pm Sat & Sun ■ ⓀⓀⓀ

Modern Swedish cuisine is served at this hotel's *(see p114)* restaurant.

The dining room at Långa Raden

8 Flickan

MAP D4 ■ Yxsmedsgränd 12 ■ 08 506 400 80 ■ Open 5pm–11pm Wed–Sat ■ ⓀⓀⓀ

Expect high-end tasting menus inspired from all over the world.

9 Den Gyldene Freden

MAP N5 ■ Österlånggatan 51 ■ 08 24 97 60 ■ Open 11:30am–midnight Mon–Fri, 1–midnight Sat ■ ⓀⓀ

Owned by the Swedish Academy, this old-fashioned, classic restaurant opened in 1722.

10 Magnus Ladulås

MAP N5 ■ Österlånggatan 26 ■ 08 21 19 57 ■ Open 11am–10pm Mon–Thu (to 11pm Fri), noon–11pm Sat ■ Ⓚ

The three-course meal offers in this cosy cellar restaurant in the heart of the Old Town are particularly good.

See map on pp84–5 ←

TOP 10 Södermalm

***Lek (Play)* (1935) by Bror Hjorth in Nytorget, SoFo**

Formerly a rough working-class district, Södermalm has been transformed by investment since 2000, blossoming into the area to see and in which to be seen. From the trendy SoFo district in the east to the hipster Hornstull at the island's western tip, "Söder" offers a blend of not-too-pricey restaurants, cool cafés, chic shopping options and a vibrant nightlife. The area has lots of greenery, and some of the best views over Stockholm – particularly from Monteliusvägen, looking across Lake Mälaren to Stadshuset. There is no shortage of museums either, notably the Fotografiska, which has earned immense international acclaim.

SÖDERMALM

Central Södermalm

- **1 Top 10 Sights** *see pp93–5*
- **1 Places to Eat** *see p97*
- **1 Cafés, Bars and Pubs** *see p96*

Söderström · Centralbron · SÖDER MÄLARSTRAND · BASTUGATAN · TAVASTGATAN · BRÄNNKYRKAGATAN · HORNSGATAN · BELLMANSGATAN · MARIA TRAPPGR. · PUSTEGRÄND · GULDGRÄND · SÖDERMALMSTORG · Slussen · KARL JOHANS TORG · Slussen · Area under redevelopment · STADSGÅRDSLEDEN · KATARINAVÄGEN · KLEVGRÄND · URVÄDERSGR. · GLASBRUKSG. · Maria-torget · TIMMERMANSG. · SANKT PAULSGATAN · SWEDENBORGSG. · BJÖRNGÅRDSGATAN · KYANGG. · FREDMANS-GATAN · KARABORGSG. · REPSLAGARGATAN · GÖTGATAN · Slussen · FISKARG. · RODDARG. · KATARINA KYRKOGÅRDSGR. · FJÄLLGATAN · STIGBERGSG. · TJÄRHOVS-PLAN · Stigbergs-parken · REBSTERNAG. · FOLKUNGAG. · BORGMÄSTARG. · MARIA PRÄSTGÅRDSGATA · HÖGBERGSGATAN · KAPELLGR. · Björns Trädgård · ÖSTGÖTAGATAN · TJÄRHOVSGATAN · BENGT EKEHJELMSG. · FATBURSGATA · FATBURS BRUNNSGATA · Fatburs-parken · FATBURSG. · Södra · SÖDERMALMSALLEN · MAGNUS LADULÅSGATAN · VÄSTGÖTAGATAN · SÖDERLEDSTUNNELN · Medborgar-platsen · FOLKUNGAGATAN · KOCKSGATAN · SÖDERMANNAG. · NYTORGSGATAN · ÅSÖGATAN · SÖDERMALM · ÅSÖGATAN · BONDEGATAN · KATARINA BANGATA · NYTORGET · SOFIAG. · MALMGÅRDSVÄGEN · Vita Bergen · BLEKINGEG. · BJURHOLMSG. · ÖSTGÖTAGATAN · BRANN ERIKSG. · GOTLANDSGATAN · KATARINA BANGATA · Bjurholm-splan · ÖLANDSG. · RINGVÄGEN · Lilla Blecktorns-parken · METARGATAN · Skanstull · RUTGER FUCHSG. · GÖTGATAN

0 metres 400 · 0 yards 400

Södermalm

Riddarfjärden · GAMLA STAN · SKEPPS-HOLMEN · Area of main map · Slussen · Mariatorget · Hornstull · Zinkensdamm · SÖDERMALM · Södra · TEGELVIKS-PLAN · Skanstull · Årstabron · Luma · Skansbron

0 km 1 · 0 miles 1

Bustling Medborgarplatsen

1 Medborgarplatsen
MAP D5

"Citizen Square" lives up to its name with a host of communal activities in and around it. In summer it comes alive with a row of outdoor bars and restaurants; in winter there is an ice-skating rink. It is also a gathering place for protests and the starting point for the May Day Parade *(see p61)*. The square is bordered by the Saluhall shopping and entertainment centre, which includes bars, good restaurants and a cinema.

2 Långholmen
MAP A4

This hilly island is a local favourite for walking, picnics, swimming and recreation. Yet from 1880 to 1975, it was home to the country's biggest prison, and Sweden's last execution took place here in 1910. The prison has been converted into a hotel and youth hostel *(see p117)*. The island has beaches and open-air stages, and is also home to Mälarvarvet, one of Stockholm's oldest shipyards.

3 SoFo
MAP D6 ■ www.sofo-stockholm.se

Short for "South of Folkungagatan", the name is a nod to the Soho districts of London and New York. The quarter is densely packed with cool, quirky and interesting shops specializing in everything from clothing and design to jewellery, vintage, homeware, music and much more. There is also a thriving restaurant and bar scene here. The last Thursday of every month is SoFo Night, when many retailers are open late and often offer special deals.

4 Monteliusvägen
MAP L6

This 500-m-(1,640-ft-) long walking path adjacent to popular Ivar Los Park offers magnificent views of Lake Mälaren, Stadshuset, Gamla Stan and Riddarholmen, especially at sunrise and sunset. Constructed in 1998 on a precipice, it has charming old houses on one side and wonderful views on the other, as well as benches and picnic tables from which to enjoy them. However, the path has areas of clay and wooden planks that can be very slippery in winter. On Blecktornsgränd, leading down to Mariatorget towards the eastern end of the walk, there are several cafés.

Canoeing off Långholmen

STIEG LARSSON'S STOCKHOLM

Södermalm became famous with the popularity of author Stieg Larsson's Millennium trilogy – particularly since the Hollywood version of *The Girl With the Dragon Tattoo* was partly filmed on Söder. The Stockholm City Museum offers "Millennium walks", and locations include Mellqvist's Kaffebar, where Larsson himself used to hang out.

5 Fotografiska

MAP E5 ■ Stadsgårdshamnen 22 ■ 08 509 005 00 ■ Open 9am–1am Thu–Sat (to 11pm Sun–Wed) ■ www.fotografiska.eu

A contemporary photography centre, Fotografiska was opened in 2010 to host works by famous photographers. The brick building that houses it was built in 1906 and formerly acted as a customs house – it now includes a bistro, café and bar.

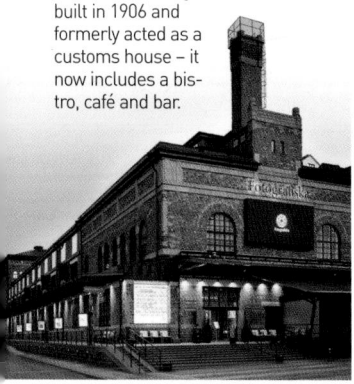

The brick exterior of Fotografiska

6 Persikan

MAP F6 ■ Tegelsviksgatan 22

A massive project called Persikan is set to transform the non-descript area beneath the SL bus depot into a showpiece of contemporary urban living. Initiated by the City of Stockholm, the project aims to develop underutilized urban spaces in a sustainable way – something that Sweden excels at. Eventually, Persikan will consist of ten apartment buildings, surrounded by shared green spaces. Work is already underway and is set to be completed in 2025. In the meantime, swing by for a glimpse of a sustainable future.

The lush and serene Mariatorget

7 Mariatorget

MAP C5

A pretty, quiet square with a gently splashing fountain, Mariatorget is a popular meeting place year round and attracts plenty of sunbathers in summer. It is the perfect spot to rest tired feet. St Paulskyrkan, a small 1876 Methodist church, faces the southwest corner of the square. Mariatorget and the streets around it, St Paulsgatan, Krukmarkargatan and Swedenborgsgatan, are popular with locals for shopping and dining.

8 Mosebacke and Mosebacke Torg

MAP D5

The district of Mosebacke has become a cultural centre thanks to Södra Teatern, which hosts music and threatrical events, and its bar. When the weather turns milder, the large open-air section of Södra Bar becomes crowded every evening. Mosebacke Torg, the square, is more peaceful – an oasis with a summer café selling cinnamon buns.

9 Skånegatan

MAP D6

The focal point of SoFo, Skånegatan is one of the city's hippest streets with designer shops and alternative bars such as Snotty Sounds Bar and Bar Agrikultur *(see p96)*. Families fill the area around Nytorget square during the day,

and it is not far to Vitabergsparken, which stages some free open-air music and dance events during the summer. Bars and restaurants in the area are lively at night, even on weekdays.

10 Tantolunden

MAP B6

People meet for swimming and picnics in this park by the waters of Årstaviken bay in summer – it can get a bit busy on sunny weekends – and for sledding in winter. There is a playground, a beach volleyball court and golf, plus cafés. The park is often used as a festival area, notably for the annual Stockholm Pride festival *(see p60)*. Away from the main areas, up the hill are more than 100 allotment gardens and cottages. The Zinkensdamm hotel and hostel *(see p117)* is in the park.

A quiet corner of Tantolunden

A DAY IN SÖDERMALM

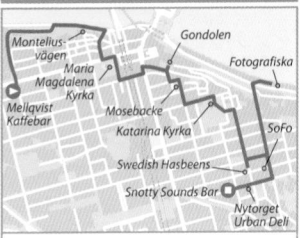

MORNING

Start the day with a cup of coffee or breakfast at **Mellqvist Kaffebar** *(see p96)* then take the short walk up Torkel Knutsonssgatan to the scenic walk along **Monteliusvägen** *(see p93)* towards Slussen. After enjoying the views across Lake Mälaren, descend to Hornsgatan and pop into 18th-century **Maria Magdalena Kyrka** *(see p41)*. Rising like a crane over Slussen is an old "lift" (no longer in use), on top of which is **Gondolen** *(see p97)*, which is quite a unique place to eat and has a good value lunchtime menu.

AFTERNOON

From Gondolen it is just a short walk to the picturesque square at **Mosebacke**. Enjoy a short, peaceful walk around the square until you reach Östgötagatan; follow it down the hill, perhaps taking a short diversion down Högbergsgatan to **Katarina Kyrka** *(see p41)* and see its attractive grounds. Cross Folkungagatan and reach the heart of **SoFo** *(see p93)*. After browsing the many design shops in the area, such as **Swedish Hasbeens** *(see p56)*, walk north-east along along Renstiernas gata, down the Söderbergs stairs to the waterfront **Fotografiska** museum on Stadsgårdshamnen. Set in the former customs house, the museum has cutting-edge international exhibits and a buzzing café. Return to Skånegatan for a delicious dinner at **Nytorget Urban Deli** *(see p97)* and maybe an after-dinner drink at **Snotty Sounds Bar** *(see p96)*.

See map on p92

Cafés, Bars and Pubs

1 Greasy Spoon

MAP E5 ■ Tjärhovsgatan 19 ■ 72 264 20 97 ■ Open 8am–4pm Mon–Fri, 9am–5pm Sat–Sun

Leading the British invasion on Södermalm, this popular brunch café *(see p53)* is the place to go for a full English, eggs Benedict or the like.

2 Morfar Ginko and Pappa Ray Ray

MAP C5 ■ Swedenborgsgatan 13 ■ 08 641 13 40 ■ Open 5pm–1am Mon–Thu & Sat, 4pm–1am Fri

Sit outside on the street front or in the cosy courtyard in summer. It serves both snacks and full meals.

3 Café & Bageri Pascal

MAP D6 ■ Skånegatan 76 ■ 08 316 110 ■ Open 7am–6pm Mon–Fri, 8am–5pm Sat–Sun

This café was opened by three siblings who share a common passion for excellent coffee. Pascal is a local favourite. It is known for its great coffee and sandwiches.

4 Häktet

MAP C5 ■ Hornsgatan 82 ■ 08 84 59 10 ■ Open 4pm–1am Mon–Wed (until 3am Thu–Sat)

A former prison turned popular late-night haunt *(see p51)* serving good food, beer, wine and cocktails.

5 Akkurat

MAP M6 ■ Hornsgatan 18 ■ Open 4pm–midnight Mon & Tue, 4pm–1am Wed & Thu, 3pm–1am Fri & Sat, 3pm–midnight Sun

Sample local Swedish brews at this excellent craft beer bar *(see p51)*.

6 Mellqvist Kaffebar

MAP C5 ■ Hornsgatan 78 ■ 07 687 529 92 ■ Open 7am–6pm Mon–Fri, 9am–6pm Sat & Sun

Renowned for its coffee, Mellqvist Kaffebar *(see p53)* also has a range of good breakfast.

Old-fashioned bar at Kvarnen

7 Kvarnen

MAP D5 ■ Tjärhovsgatan 4 ■ 08 643 03 80 ■ Open 11am–1am Mon & Tue (to 3am Wed–Sat), noon–11pm Sun

An old-fashioned Swedish beer hall, Kvarnen *(see p50)* becomes a popular bar-nightclub on weekends.

8 Babylon

MAP D5 ■ Björns Trädgårdsgränd ■ 08 640 80 83 ■ Open 11am–midnight Mon–Fri

Hidden in a park just across the road from bustling Medborgarplatsen, Babylon has a long, narrow bar that is perfect for almost any occasion at any time of the day or year.

9 Snotty Sounds Bar

MAP D6 ■ Skånegatan 90 ■ 08 644 39 10 ■ Open 4pm–1am daily

Probably the only "hole in the wall" music bar *(see p50)* in the city, Snotty has pictures of new wave and punk icons on the walls and plays tunes to match. It is small and can get very crowded at weekends.

10 Johan & Nyström

MAP C5 ■ Swedenborgsgatan 7 ■ 08 530 22 440 ■ Open 7am–7:30pm Mon–Fri, 8am–7:30pm Sat & Sun

The concept store of these specialist coffee roasters *(see p52)* is a must visit for anyone serious about the black stuff.

See map on p92

Places to Eat

PRICE CATEGORIES

For a three-course meal for one with half a bottle of wine (or equivalent meal), taxes and extra charges.

Ⓚ under 700 kr ⓀⓀ 700–1,000 kr ⓀⓀⓀ over 1,000 kr

1 Calexico's

MAP A5 ■ Hornstulls Strand 4 ■ 08 658 63 50 ■ Open 5pm–11pm Tue–Thu, 5pm–1am Fri & Sat, 11am–4pm Sun ■ Ⓚ

Organic Cal-Mex cuisine and great cocktails are served here *(see p54)*.

2 Meatballs for the People

MAP D5 ■ Nytorgsgatan 30 ■ 08 466 60 99 ■ Open 11am–9pm Sun–Thu (to 11pm Fri & Sat) ■ Ⓚ

Classic Swedish food is done 14 different ways at this spot *(see p55)*.

3 Nytorget Urban Deli

MAP E6 ■ Nytorget 4 ■ 08 599 091 80 ■ Open 8am–11pm Sun–Tue (to midnight Wed & Thu, to 1am Fri & Sat) ■ ⓀⓀ

A restaurant, bar and food store *(see p54)* with a lively New York feel.

4 Vina

MAP E6 ■ Sofiagatan 1 ■ 70 406 66 26 ■ Open 5–10pm Tue–Thu, 4–11pm Fri, 2–11pm Sat ■ ⓀⓀ

This restaurant serves tapas, seasonal dishes and excellent natural wines.

5 Gondolen

MAP D5 ■ Stadsgården 6 ■ 08 641 70 90 ■ Open L: 11:30am–2:30pm Mon–Fri; D: 5–11pm Mon, 5pm–1am Tue–Fri, 4pm–1am Sat ■ ⓀⓀⓀ

Fine-dining atop Katarinahissen, a Stockholm landmark.

6 Tjoget

MAP A5 ■ Hornsbruksgatan 24 ■ 08 22 00 21 ■ Open 4pm–1am Mon–Thu, 4pm–3am Fri, noon–3am Sat, noon–1am Sun ■ ⓀⓀ

Continental European cocktail bar and restaurant, popular with the after-work crowd for refreshers or late nights out in the increasingly fashionable Hornstull area.

7 Punk Royale

MAP E5 ■ Folkungagatan 128 ■ Open 5:30pm–midnight Tue–Fri (from 3pm Sat) ■ Online reservations only ■ ⓀⓀⓀ

A young maverick on the Stockholm dining scene, Punk Royale *(see p55)* tears up the rule book with edgy dishes in a high-energy environment.

8 Deli Di Luca

MAP E5 ■ Folkungagatan 110 ■ 08 644 04 20 ■ Open 11am–10pm Mon & Tue (to 11pm Wed–Fri), noon–11pm Sat ■ Ⓚ

A taste of Italy with a Nordic twist. Sit in for or a meal or buy ingredients to take away for a picnic.

9 Hermans

MAP E5 ■ Fjällgatan 23b ■ 08 643 94 80 ■ Open 11am–10pm daily ■ Ⓚ

With an all-you-can-eat vegetarian buffet, Hermans offers great variety.

10 Pelikan

MAP D6 ■ Blekingegatan 40 ■ 08 556 090 90 ■ Open 5pm–midnight Mon–Thu, 1pm–1am Fri & Sat (to 11pm Sun) ■ Ⓚ

Enjoy traditional Swedish food in a 17th-century beer hall setting.

Traditional interior of Pelikan

TOP 10 Further Afield

It is easy to venture beyond Stockholm – and there is plenty to see. SL Access cards are of great value for those who want to roam as the Greater Stockholm travel card zone extends to the port of Nynäshamn in the south and beyond Norrtälje in the north. Buses usually run to the most out-of-the-way sights, even the wilderness of Tyresö National Park. The city of Uppsala is one of the best day trips from the city, as is the Stockholm Archipelago.

Beautiful Uppsala

FURTHER AFIELD

Järlåsa
Uppsala
Almunge
Erken
Rörsby
Källinge
Husby-Långhundra
Rimbo
Örsundsbro
Ekoln
Dillingby
Arlanda
Kårsta
Enköping
Grillby
Märsta
Sigtuna
Lindholmen
Roslags-Kulla
35 km (22 miles)
Lillkyrka
Bålsta
Rosersberg
Vallentuna
Upplands-Väsby
N. Ljusterн
Oknön
Bro
Åkersberga
Kungsängen
Sollentuna
Täby
S. Ljusterн
Bogesunds-landet
Resaro
Grinн
Mälaren
Munsö
Järfälla
Naturhistoriska riksmuseet
Selaön
Adelsö
Färingsö
Hagaparken
Millesgården
Värmdö
Mälaren
Bromma
Drottningholm
Stockholm
Värmeland
Birka
Björkö
Ekerö
Mariefred
Globen
Saltsjöbaden
Ingar
Ekeby
Botkyrka
Tyresö
Huddinge
Brevik
Nykvarn
Rönninge
Tumba
Handen
Södertälje
Jordbro
Tungelsta
Västerhaninge
Dalarö
Gålö
Ornö
0 km 12
0 miles 12

1 Hagaparken

This "English Park" *(see pp34–5)* has softly shaped lawns interspersed with dark forests where paths meander amidst elegant trees, and with pavilions and ruins offering constant surprises. It lies just north of the city and is easily reached by bus.

2 Uppsala

Sweden's fourth-biggest city and a major university town founded in 1477, Uppsala is picturesque and lively, with a striking cathedral. SL commuter trains take under an hour from Stockholm to Uppsala station, right in the city centre.

3 Sigtuna

Founded in 980, Sigtuna is Sweden's oldest city. It has a popular centre, with low wooden houses, lots of cafés, craft shops and a charming museum. There are also the ruins of two churches – St Olof's and St Per's. The city can be reached by local train to Märsta followed by a connecting bus ride. Boat trips to Sigtuna operate from Stockholm during the summer, travelling through Lake Mälaren.

Ruins of St Olof's church, Sigtuna

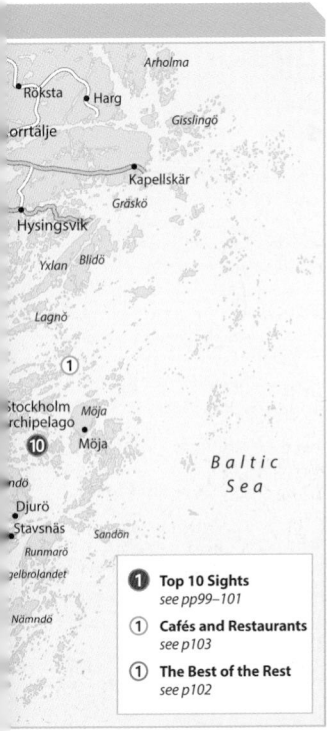

4 Naturhistoriska Riksmuseet

MAP C1 ■ Frescativägen 40 ■ 08 519 540 40 ■ Open 10am–6pm Tue–Sun ■ Adm ■ www.nrm.se

The natural sciences are presented in a lively and interactive manner at this natural history museum. Varied exhibits showcase everything from the history of life and the origin of species to visits to polar regions and the treasures of the earth's interior. Adventures with dinosaurs and in outer space come to life at the IMAX cinema, Cosmonova *(see p49)*.

Exhibit at Naturhistoriska Riksmuseet

Drottningholm palace and gardens

CARL MILLES

One of Sweden's most famous sculptors, Carl Milles (1875–1955) was an assistant to French sculptor Auguste Rodin in Paris and spent over 20 years in the United States – many major municipal buildings in America include his sculptures. Milles and his wife Olga acquired the house at Millesgården in 1906, and its spacious terraces were developed over the next 50 years.

5 Drottningholm

One of the best day trips from Stockholm, Drottningholm's *(see pp24–5)* Royal Palace and its park is one of three UNESCO World Heritage sites in and around the city.

6 Millesgården

Herserudsvägen 32, Lidingö ■ www.millesgarden.se

This spectacular park overlooking the water includes sculptor Carl Milles's most famous works arranged on terraces below his former home. In 1936, Carl and his wife Olga donated Millesgården to the Swedes; castings of some of his sculptures are still sold in very limited editions to help fund the property's upkeep. Millesgården is an easy and pleasant trip from Stockholm; take the tram from Ropsten.

7 Birka

A UNESCO World Heritage Site, Birka is one of the most complete examples of a Viking trading settlement from around the 8th and 9th centuries. While practically nothing remains above ground of what existed during that era, a museum illustrates how the town looked and functioned, and there are some remarkable finds here. The island itself is calm and unspoilt with sheep and bull calves roaming about. Birka can be reached by boat trips in the summer.

Viking coin, Birka

8 Mariefred

Dominated by the fairytale-like Gripsholm Castle, the charming town of Mariefred is characterized by narrow streets and low wooden buildings in soft colours, mostly dating from the 18th and 19th centuries. It is a popular day trip; in summer take the steamboat, S/S *Mariefred*, from Stadshuskajen, next to Stadshuset. It is also possible to take a train from Stockholm to Läggesta and change to the Östra Södermalms steam railway to Mariefred (summer only). Combine the trip here with a visit to the Taxinge Slott *(see p102)*.

Gripsholm Castle, Mariefred

9 Ericsson Globen

Globentorget 2 ■ 07 718 110 00 ■ Open 10am–6pm Mon–Fri (to 4pm Sat & Sun); extended opening hours in summer ■ Adm: Skyview ■ www.globearenas.se

Not only is Globen *(see p47)* an excellent indoor arena for sport and concerts, but also the largest spherical building in the world. The white ball can be seen for miles around – and it is possible to travel to the top and enjoy great views through the glass gondolas running on tracks fixed to the globe's exterior. The trip is always a popular one – even weddings take place in the gondolas – so book ahead.

Rödlöga, Stockholm Archipelago

10 Stockholm Archipelago

One could spend a few weeks exploring Stockholm's wonderful archipelago *(see pp16–17)*, but it is still possible to sample many of its delights even on a short trip. The main town on the archipelago is Vaxholm, with its well-preserved wooden houses dating from the turn of the 19th century, painted in delicate pastel tones. There are charming harbour-side restaurants and cafés, and it is easily accessible year round, by Waxholmsbolagets boat or by bus 670 from Stockholm.

DAY TRIP TO UPPSALA

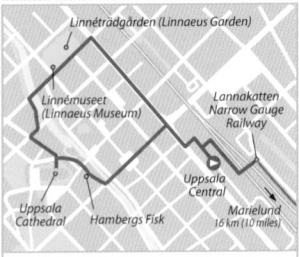

MORNING

Uppsala *(see p99)* is perfect for a day trip, with most of its sights concentrated in the historic western side of the city. The centre of town is within easy walking distance from the central railway station. On arrival, turn right out of the station; it is a short walk to the north to the beautifully laid-out **Linnéträdgården (Linnaeus Garden)** and **Linnémuseet (Linnaeus Museum)**. Cross the river and swing back along its course to the **Uppsala Cathedral**, dating back to the 13th century and the tallest church building in Scandinavia. King Gustav Vasa is buried here. **Hambergs Fisk** *(see p103)* is just a stone's throw from the cathedral, and as one of the best-rated restaurants in the city, an ideal stop for lunch. Its menu offers excellent value compared to the evening à la carte dishes.

AFTERNOON

On the eastern side of Uppsala station is the terminus of the **Lennakatten Narrow Gauge Railway** *(see p102)*. The 32-km (20-mile) route wends through forests and past lakes, with six different station stops: for a return trip to Marielund allow around two hours, which will give ample time for a stroll and refreshments in the station café. From Uppsala there are regular trains for Stockholm (around three direct trains per hour until late evening). If you are staying here for dinner, the last direct train to Stockholm from Uppsala station departs at around 10pm.

See map on pp98–9

The Best of the Rest

1 Torekällberget Outdoor Museum, Södertälje

Torekällberget,151 89 Södertälje ■ 08 523 014 22 ■ Open Sep–May: 10am–4pm daily (Jun–Aug: to 5pm daily)

The museum houses a charming village, exhibitions and animals that were once common on local farms.

2 Steninge Slott

Steninge Slottsväg 141, 195 91 Märsta ■ Train from Stockholm to Märsta, then bus 584 to Steninge ■ 08 592 595 00 ■ Open 11am–6pm Mon–Fri, 10am–5pm Sat & Sun

This Baroque palace is located by the waters of Lake Mälaren near Sigtuna. It hosts a Christmas market.

3 Lennakatten Narrow Gauge Railway, Uppsala

Uppsala Östra station, Uppsala ■ 01 813 05 00 ■ Open Jun–early Sep ■ Adm ■ www.lennakatten.se

Ride this steam train from Uppsala through dense forests and lakes.

Tyresta National Park at dawn

4 Tyresta National Park

Tyresta village, 136 59 Vendelsö ■ 08 745 33 94

Just 20 km (12 miles) from central Stockholm, this is a vast area of unspoiled beauty, superb for hiking.

5 Björnö

MAP H2 ■ Buses 428 & 429

Located on Ingarö island, this nature reserve has beaches and camping.

Free-fall ride at Tom Tits Experiment

6 Tom Tits Experiment, Södertälje

Storgatan 33, 151 36 Södertälje ■ 08 550 225 00 ■ Open 10am–5pm daily ■ Adm

Spend at least half a day in this interactive science museum, which has attractions for all ages.

7 Saltsjöbaden

Take the Saltsjöbanan light train to this beautiful seaside resort. An organic café, Stationhuset, sells lunches and snacks year round.

8 Skogskyrkogården

Skogskyrkogården ■ 08 508 317 30

Actress Greta Garbo is buried in this cemetery, which is a UNESCO World Heritage Site.

9 Taxinge Slott

Taxinge Slott, Taxinge ■ 01 597 01 14 ■ www.taxingeslott.se

This castle is famous for its cake buffet featuring an impressive 65 types of locally baked cakes.

10 Västerås

One of Sweden's oldest cities, Västerås has many museums, shops, a cathedral and a botanic garden.

See map on pp98–9

Cafés and Restaurants

1 Finnhamns Café & Krog

Finnhamns brygga ■ 08 542 464 12 ■ Open Jun–Aug: 11:30am–3pm & 5pm–late daily; May, Sep–Oct: 11am–midnight Sat & Sun ■ Ⓚ

Enjoy a glass of wine and sumptuous dishes while taking in the great views.

2 Nya Carnegiebryggeriet

Ljusslingan 15–17 ■ 08 510 650 82 ■ Open 4–11pm Tue–Fri, 3pm–1am Sat ■ Ⓚ

A must-visit for craft-beer lovers, this is a brewery, bar and restaurant in the Hammarby Sjöstad district.

3 Båthuset

Hamnen, Sigtuna ■ 07 217 464 54 ■ Open May–Sep: 6–10pm Tue–Sat; Oct–Apr: to 9pm Wed–Sat ■ Ⓚ

This floating restaurant exudes quality and has a homely ambience.

4 Vaxholms Hembygdsgårds Café

Trädgårdsgatan 19, Vaxholm ■ 08 541 319 80 ■ Open weekends in May, daily Jun–mid-Sep ■ Ⓚ

A pretty waterfront café serving light Swedish food such as salads, waffles, pancakes and open sandwiches.

5 Hambergs Fisk

Fyristorg 8, Uppsala ■ 01 871 21 50 ■ Open 11:30am–10pm Tue–Sat ■ Ⓚ

This small seafood restaurant has a French bistro-like atmosphere.

6 Landet

LM Ericssons väg 27, Telefonplan ■ 08 410 193 20 ■ Open 4–11pm Mon–Tue (to midnight Wed & Thu, 1am Fri & Sat) ■ Ⓚ

Landet *(see p51)* is a restaurant, bar, club and live music venue in one.

PRICE CATEGORIES

For a three-course meal for one, with half a bottle of wine (or equivalent meal), taxes and extra charges.

Ⓚ under 700 kr ⓀⓀ 700–1,000 kr
ⓀⓀⓀ over 1,000 kr

7 Sjöpaviljongen

Traneberg Strand 4, Bromma ■ 08 704 04 24 ■ Open 11:15am–10pm Mon–Fri, noon–10pm Sat (to 9pm Sun) ■ Ⓚ

Set in lovely waterside surroundings, Sjöpaviljongen has a terrace to eat on in the summer.

8 Stationshuset i Saltsjöbaden

Saltsjöbaden station ■ 08 556 266 00 ■ Open 9am–5pm daily ■ Ⓚ

Organic food is served in this former station house, where trains heading here from Slussen terminate.

9 Skärgårdskrogen i Saltsjöbaden

Vikingavägen 17a, Saltsjöbaden ■ 08 717 15 60 ■ Open Sep–Apr: 10:30am–2pm Mon–Fri; May–Aug: 10:30am–late daily ■ Ⓚ

A true archipelago dining experience just a short train from Slussen. Open for lunch all-year round.

10 Rökeriet, Fjärderholmarna

Fjärderholmarna ■ 08 716 50 88 ■ Open May–early Sep: noon–10pm daily ■ Ⓚ

An idyllic archipelago restaurant, Rökeriet specializes in seafood.

The waterside Rökeriet

Streetsmart

Brunkebergstunneln, a brightly coloured pedestrian tunnel

Getting Around	**106**
Practical Information	**108**
Places to Stay	**112**
General Index	**118**
Acknowledgments	**124**
Phrase Book	**126**

Getting Around

Arriving by Air

Arlanda Airport is the major international airport in the region, set 37 km (23 miles) north of Stockholm. Direct flights to European and North American destinations are served by the likes of **British Airways**, **KLM**, **Lufthansa**, **Norwegian Air** and **SAS**. Terminals 2 and 5 serve all international flights; domestic flights depart from terminals 3 and 4.

It's easy to get from the airport to the city – the **Arlanda Express** airport train will whisk you to the centre in just 20 minutes. Alternatively, take the cheaper SL commuter train from Arlanda Central Station (between terminals 4 and 5), which takes around 40 minutes to reach Stockholm Central Station. The airport coach services also take around 40 minutes. Taxis will go to any city centre destination for a fixed fee.

Stockholm Skavsta Airport, also known as Nyköping Airport, some 100 km (62 miles) south of Stockholm, is Sweden's main airport for low-cost, no-frills carriers. It caters to flights from several European destinations. Access to Stockholm is via a coach service that takes 80–90 minutes. Alternatively, take a train from nearby Nyköping.

Arriving by Train

Stockholm Central Station is the main rail hub for both intercity and local rail services. There is also a daily express service, which runs every two hours to and from Copenhagen in Denmark via Malmö in Sweden.

The state-owned **Statens Järnvägar** (SJ) runs most of the intercity routes, though there are some private train operators. The lowest fares can be purchased 90 days in advance. Suburban commuter trains are run by the city's local transport authority, **Storstockholms Lokaltrafik** (SL). SL travel cards and tickets are valid on these services.

Arriving by Road

The Öresund toll bridge connects Denmark and Sweden. From there, follow the E4 – a 550-km (340-mile) continuous motorway – to Stockholm. Driving around the centre is not recommended: leave your car in a secure long-stay car park and explore the city on foot or by public transport.

Arriving By Boat

Ferries from Finland (Helsinki and Turku), Estonia (Tallinn) and Latvia (Riga) to Stockholm are operated by two companies, **Tallink Silja Line** (whose ships dock at Värtahamnen in the north east of the city) and **Viking Line** (whose ships dock at Stadsgården, right at the northern edge of the Södermalm area).

Getting Around by Local Train

Local trains are cheap and handy for several destinations further afield. The *pendeltåg* (commuter train) network extends from Nynäshamn, 60 km (37 miles) south of the city, to Märsta, near Arlanda Airport, and to the nearby city of Uppsala. The Saltsjöbadan suburban rail provides an easy connection between the city and the Saltsjöbaden area of the Stockholm Archipelago, while the narrow-gauge Roslagsbanan network serves 39 destinations northeast of Stockholm.

Getting Around by Metro

The underground *tunnelbana* (or T-bana) is the fastest way to get around town. There are three lines – red, green and blue. Trains run until around midnight on weekdays, and all night on Fridays, Saturdays and the eve of most public holidays.

As with all modes of local transport operated by SL, including buses, trams and the Djurgården ferry, nearly all tickets for the metro can be loaded on to an SL Access card – an electronic smart card. You need to pay a fee for the card itself, but you can reuse your card on future visits. There are also single-use travel cards valid for 75 minutes, and 24 or 72 hours.

You can also use contactless credit and debit cards in the same way as the SL Access card. As discounts aren't available for contactless payments, it is usually cheaper to use a SL

Access card, travel card or paper ticket.

Tickets and travel cards are sold at Pressbyrån convenience stores (found at many stations), at the SL Center at T-Centralen metro station and at metro and commuter railway stations. There are also ticket machines at most metro and commuter railway stations.

Getting Around by Bus and Tram

The city has an extensive bus network. While most services operate until around midnight, some major routes run all night. There are night bus services seven days a week to many destinations further afield.

The tram network, largely dismantled in 1967, has made a comeback. Line 7N, which runs between the centre and Waldemarsudde, has been reopened to regular traffic. There is still a vintage tram that runs from spring to autumn.

Getting Around by Car

Driving in the centre is discouraged. A congestion tax is levied on vehicles, and parking is expensive and difficult to find. There are 25 park-and-ride stops on the way to central Stockholm to promote the usage of public transport.

Sweden has very tough laws on drinking and driving *(see p108)*.

Getting Around by Taxi

Taxis are expensive – a trip from a suburb to the city centre may cost around 400 kr; a short hop across town will rarely be under 250 kr. Reputable companies include **Taxi Stockholm**, **Taxi 020** and **Taxi Kurir**.

Getting Around by Boat

Boats link the city to sights in Lake Mälaren and islands in the archipelago. You can travel to Djurgården on a ferry from Slussen in just 10 minutes (an SL pass is valid). Most services are operated by **Waxholmsbolaget**.

Getting Around by Bicycle

Although it is easy to pedal around the city because of its network of bike lanes, the conditions can be difficult in winter. Hire bikes for three days or for the season with **City Bikes** from April to October.

Getting Around on Foot

Walking is a great way to explore Stockholm. It has wide pavements, the distances between many *tunnelbana* stations are relatively short and vehicles are always obliged to stop at road crossings. Pathways along quaysides, in parks and esplanades are also shared with cyclists; be sure to stay on the pedestrian side.

DIRECTORY

ARRIVING BY AIR

Arlanda Airport
W arlanda.se/en

Arlanda Express
W arlandaexpress.com

British Airways
W britishairways.com

KLM
W klm.com

Lufthansa
W lufthansa.com

Norwegian Air
W norwegian.com

SAS
W sas.se/en

Stockholm Skavsta Airport
W skavsta.se/en

ARRIVING BY TRAIN

Statens Järnvägar
W sj.se

Stockholm Central Station
W dinstation.se/stockholms-centralstation

Storstockholms Lokaltrafik
W sl.se

ARRIVING BY BOAT

Tallink Silja Line
W tallinksilja.com

Viking Line
W vikingline.se

GETTING AROUND BY TAXI

Taxi 020
W taxi020.se

Taxi Kurir
W taxikurir.se

Taxi Stockholm
W taxistockholm.se

GETTING AROUND BY BOAT

Waxholmsbolaget
W waxholmsbolaget.se

GETTING AROUND BY BICYCLE

City Bikes
W citybikes.se

Practical Information

Passports and Visas

For entry requirements, including visas, consult your nearest Swedish embassy or check the **Migrationsverket** (Swedish Migration Agency) or **Visit Sweden** websites. Citizens of the UK, US, Canada, Australia and New Zealand do not need visas for stays of up to three months but, from late 2023, must apply in advance for the European Travel Information and Authorization System (**ETIAS**). Visitors from other countries may also require an ETIAS, so check before travelling. EU nationals do not need a visa or an ETIAS.

A number of countries including the UK, US and Australia have consulates in Sweden and are able to provide limited consular services to their nationals.

Government Advice

Now more than ever, it is important to consult both your and the Swedish government's advice before travelling. The **UK Foreign, Commonwealth & Development Office (FCDO)**, the **US Department of State**, the **Australian Department of Foreign Affairs and Trade** and **Visit Sweden** offer the latest information on security, health and local regulations.

Customs Information

You can find information on the laws relating to goods and currency taken in or out of Sweden on the **Tullverket** website. There are no restrictions for EU citizens if goods are for personal use. Arrivals from outside the EU can import a litre of spirits, four litres of wine or 16 litres of beer, plus 200 cigarettes, 50 cigars, or 250g of tobacco.

Insurance

We recommend that you take out a comprehensive insurance policy covering theft, loss of belongings, medical care, cancellations and delays, and read the small print carefully.

The UK has a reciprocal healthcare agreement with Sweden, meaning that UK citizens pay the same fee for medical treatment as locals provided they have a valid European Health Insurance Card (EHIC) or UK Global Health Insurance Card (**GHIC**). Australia has a similar reciprocal health care agreement with Sweden and citizens can access essential medical treatment as long as they are registered to **Medicare**. As not all treatments are covered by these agreements, separate insurance is also advisable.

Health

Sweden has a world-class healthcare system, but medical care comes at a cost, even for citizens. If you have an EHIC or GHIC, be sure to present this as soon as possible to take advantage of reduced fees. For other visitors, payment of medical expenses is the patient's responsibility. It is therefore important to arrange comprehensive medical insurance before travelling to Sweden.

Swedish hospitals are excellent. A list of doctors is available on the **Healthcare Guide 1177** website. If you need a dentist, **City Dental**, in the city centre, is open all week, and most staff speak English.

Regulations governing the sales of pharmaceuticals in Sweden are strict; a prescription is required to purchase medicines that can be bought over the counter in many other countries.

Those who hike, camp or take outdoor activities in wooded regions or city parks should take measures to prevent tick bites – a risk of tick-borne encephalitis is present throughout the countryside including the Stockholm archipelago.

For information regarding COVID-19 vaccination requirements, consult government advice.

Unless stated otherwise, tap water in Sweden is safe to drink.

Smoking, Alcohol and Drugs

Smoking in Swedish bars and restaurants has been banned since 2005, but additional laws now limit smoking in public places, including in playgrounds, railway stations, and in outdoor sections of restaurants and bars.

Beware of the strict rules regarding alcohol,

drugs and some medications when driving. A driver is guilty of drunk driving with a blood alcohol level of only 0.2 per mil. Gross drunk driving (from 1.0 per mil) is punishable by imprisonment.

The possession of drugs is illegal and the country's marijuana laws are some of the harshest in Europe; the country outright bans any and all possession and sale, including medical marijuana, with few exceptions.

ID

Visitors are not required to carry passports or ID cards on their person but, in the case of an incident, you must be able to produce suitable identification at a police station within 12 hours.

Personal Security

Stockholm is generally a very safe city, and no unusual precautions are necessary except common sense. Pickpockets are the greatest hazard; always keep your valuables safe, since fairly brazen attempts at theft in crowded bars are not uncommon. The weekend drinking crowd can get rowdy late at night around Medborgarplatsen and Stureplan, and in metro stations, but is generally harmless if ignored. Busy nightlife areas and the larger metro stations are usually well policed.

There is one **emergency number** for all services; it will work regardless of whether or not you have international roaming or phone credit. All operators speak English, and interpretation services are also available. You can also contact the police in a **non-emergency**. Crimes such as theft should be reported to the police for insurance purposes – you will then be provided with the necessary documentation. The Swedish police are friendly and helpful, and most of them speak fluent English.

Contact your embassy if you have your passport stolen, or in the event of a serious crime or accident.

As a rule, Swedes are very accepting of all people, regardless of their race, gender or sexuality. Homosexuality has been legal here since 1944, and the age of consent was equalized in 1972. The Swedish parliament voted to make same-sex marriages legal in 2009 by an overwhelming majority of 261 to 22. Sweden hosts a number of LGBTQ+ events annually, including more Pride festivals per capita than in anywhere else in the world, and the Gay Happiness Index ranks Sweden consistently high, alongside its Scandinavian neighbours. If you do feel unsafe at anytime while you're in Stockholm, contact **Stockholm LGBT** for support and advice.

DIRECTORY

PASSPORTS AND VISAS

ETIAS
W etiasvisa.com

Migrationsverket
W migrationsverket.se

Visit Sweden
W visitsweden.com/passport-and-visas

GOVERNMENT ADVICE

Australian Department of Foreign Affairs and Trade
W dfat.gov.au
W smartraveller.gov.au

UK Foreign, Commonwealth & Development Office (FCDO)
W gov.uk/foreign-travel-advice

US Department of State
W travel.state.gov

Visit Stockholm
W visitstockholm.com

CUSTOMS INFORMATION

Tullverket
W tullverket.se

INSURANCE

GHIC
W ghic.org.uk

Medicare
W servicesaustralia.gov.au/medicare

HEALTH

City Dental
W citydental.se

Healthcare Guide 1177
W 1177.se

PERSONAL SECURITY

Emergency
C 112

Non-Emergency
C 114 14

Stockholm LGBT
W stockholmlgbt.com

Travellers With Specific Requirements

Stockholm prides itself on being one of the most accessible capital cities in the world. The metro and local trains are adapted for users with specific requirements, with access at all stations, and buses "kneel" at stops to help travellers board and disembark. Additionally, around 360 bus stops in the city have been modified by raising the kerb height. All buses have wheelchair ramps.

Public areas have to be accessible for physically or visually disabled people, as well as those suffering from allergies. All new buildings have wheelchair ramps and spacious toilets for people with mobility issues, and most historic attractions have step-free access and disabled toilets. For more detailed information, visit the **De Handikappades Riksförbund** (National Disabled Association) or the **Visit Sweden** website.

Time Zone

Stockholm is on Central European Time (CET), one hour ahead of Greenwich Mean Time (GMT) and six hours ahead of US Eastern Standard Time. Swedish summer time begins on the last Sunday in March and ends on the last Sunday in October.

Money

Sweden's currency is the Swedish krona (SEK or kr, plural kronor). Sweden is fast on its way to becoming a fully cashless society with only one per cent of payments now made with cash. Credit cards and debit cards are often the only accepted mode of payment, and are used even for small transactions. Avoid taking out large amounts of cash in advance of your trip – you may find yourself unable to spend it.

Electrical Appliances

Electricity is 220V and the socket is for the standard continental Europe plug (type C and F). Visitors bringing electrical devices from the UK will need a continental adaptor plug. American appliances will need a transformer.

Mobile Phones and Wi-Fi

Mobile phone reception is good throughout the city, even on the underground rail system. As a rule, travellers from the EU can use their data allowance without being charged an additional fee. However, it is wise to contact your phone provider prior to travelling to clarify whether international roaming is activated on your mobile. To avoid roaming fees if you are visiting from outside the EU, buy a local operator's pay-as-you-go SIM card and some credit.

Most people's homes in Stockholm have high-speed broadband, so internet cafés have never really caught on here. Free Wi-Fi access is available almost everywhere, including cafés, bars, restaurants and hotels.

Post

The national post office, **PostNord** has leased most of its counter operations to private shops – look out for the blue and yellow PostNord symbol outside newsagents or supermarkets. Stamps are available from Pressbyrån or 7/11 stores. Postboxes are yellow for national and international mail; blue for mail for the Stockholm postcode areas (100–199). The last collections are usually at around 5pm.

Weather

Stockholm is a city of wild climatic contrasts. The summer can be unusually warm – hot even – with al fresco dining the norm. Spring and autumn are both quite brief. Wrap up for winter – the temperature can drop as low as -20° C (-4° F) and some years it rarely rises above zero in the months between November and March.

May through August is the high season, but the city is never overcrowded – in high summer you may have some areas almost to yourself as the locals head for the countryside. September is great, with blue skies and pretty foliage. December to February is also a delightful time to visit, even if it gets dark around mid-afternoon.

Opening Hours

Most tourist attractions and major museums are open all day year-round, though be aware that opening hours are often shorter during the winter months, and some outdoor attractions such as Gröna Lund are only open in spring and summer. Major shops are typically open every day of the year, with business hours of somewhere between roughly 8am and 7pm.

Some restaurants and bars only open in the evenings, and will be closed altogether in the early part of the week. Most city centre bars stay open until midnight or 1am. Late-night bars and clubs stay open until 2am or 3am (a handful until 5am).

The two public holidays always liable to upset the norm regarding opening hours are Christmas and Midsummer *(see p61)* – most establishments will be closed on these dates. In the weeks either side of these dates, it is normal that a few shops, bars and restaurants will be closed for a few days or even a week or two.

The COVID-19 pandemic proved that situations can change suddenly. Always check before visiting attractions and hospitality venues for up-to-date hours and booking requirement.

Visitor Information

The main tourist office is at Kulturhuset on Sergels torg, a five-minute walk from Stockholm Central Station. It is well stocked with guides, maps and leaflets. **Sweden.se**, the official site for information about Sweden, is good for travel and tourism advice. It is entirely multilingual, as is the **Visit Stockholm** site. The Visit Sweden site is also a useful resource, and is available in English, Dutch, German and French.

The **Stockholm Pass** grants discounts for events, museum entry, guided tours, activities and transport. As this card is not free, it is worth carefully considering how many of the offers you are likely to take advantage of before purchasing one for the duration of your stay.

Local Customs

Swedes are pretty casual. The use of first names is the norm and a friendly "Hej!" is the common greeting. Casual clothing is acceptable almost everywhere, including restaurants. One Swedish drinking custom to watch out for is the tradition of "skåling", which confounds many. To "skål", look the person in the eye, raise your glass, drink, then repeat the eye contact before putting your glass down.

Language

Swedish is the official language of Sweden, while five national minority languages are also recognized by law. These are Finnish, Yiddish, Meänkieli, Romani and Sami. Additionally, a number of indigenous languages are spoken. In Stockholm, English is widely understood and spoken.

Taxes and Refunds

The standard VAT rate in Sweden is 25 per cent, making it one of the highest in the world, with reduced rates of 12 per cent and 6 per cent for food, books, newspapers, and other goods and services. If you reside outside the EU and are leaving Europe, you can get a refund for the items you purchased in Sweden via **Global Blue** before departing from an international airport.

Accommodation

Hotels in Stockholm do not come cheap, but the upside is that standards are good across the city and beyond. Thanks to a reliable public transport system that runs all night at weekends, travellers on a budget can consider cheaper options outside the centre, as well as a hostel or a B&B.

DIRECTORY

TRAVELLERS WITH SPECIFIC REQUIREMENTS

De Handikappades Riksförbund
W dhr.se

Visit Sweden
W visitsweden.com/accessible-travel

POST

PostNord
W postnord.se/en

VISITOR INFORMATION

Stockholm Pass
W stockholmpass.com

Sweden.se
W sweden.se

Visit Stockholm
W visitstockholm.com

TAXES AND REFUNDS

Global Blue
W globalblue.com

Places to Stay

PRICE CATEGORIES
For a standard double room and taxes per night during the high season. Breakfast is not included unless specified.

(Kr) under 1,500 (Kr)(Kr) 1,500–2,500 (Kr)(Kr)(Kr) over 2,500

High-End Hotels

Grand Central by Scandic

MAP K2 ■ Kungsgatan 70 ■ 08 512 520 00 ■ www.scandichotels.com ■ (Kr)
Housed in a 130-year-old building, the classy Grand Central by Scandic is centrally located close to the railway station and the Arlanda Express *(see p106)*. The hotel has a music focus – guests can order in-room concerts, and there are stages throughout the hotel with live music and DJs every night of the week.

Clarion Sign

MAP K3 ■ Östra Järnvägsgatan 35 ■ 08 676 98 00 ■ www.nordicchoicehotels.com ■ (Kr)(Kr)
This city-centre hotel reflects the Scandinavian spirit with its classic furniture and black-and-white photographs. The Clarion Sign also has a spa - with a gym, sauna and heated outdoor pool - all with fantastic views across Stockholm.

First Hotel Reisen

MAP N5 ■ Skeppsbron 12 ■ 08 22 32 60 ■ www.firsthotels.com ■ (Kr)(Kr)
With its great waterside setting close to the Royal Palace, the Reisen is a classic hotel with a maritime theme. All of the standard rooms have views of the Old Town, while the superior rooms look out across the waterfront, and luxury rooms have saunas, Jacuzzis and balconies.

Radisson Blu Waterfront Hotel

MAP K4 ■ Nils Ericssons Plan 4 ■ 08 505 060 00 ■ www.radissonblu.com ■ (Kr)(Kr)
Close to Stockholm Central Station, this hotel is connected to the 3,000-seater Stockholm Waterfront Congress Centre, and is popular for major business functions. The rooms offer views over the city and waterfront. Breakfast is included.

Elite Eden Park

MAP N1 ■ Sturegatan 22 ■ 08 555 627 00 ■ www.elite.se/eng/edenpark ■ (Kr)(Kr)(Kr)
Ideally located between Stureplan's nightlife district and the peaceful Humlegården, this hotel has an English-style gastropub and an Asian restaurant. There are 124 comfortable rooms, a gymnasium and a sauna. Breakfast is included.

Ett Hem

MAP C1 ■ Sköldungagatan 2 ■ 08 20 05 90 ■ www.etthem.se ■ (Kr)(Kr)(Kr)
Luxury central living is what is on offer at Ett Hem, a boutique hotel in a 20th-century former townhouse with green gardens. Each of its 12 rooms is individually decorated with classic Scandinavian furniture, antiques and design.

Grand Hotel

MAP N4 ■ Södra Blasieholmshammen 8 ■ 08 679 35 00 ■ www.grandhotel.se ■ (Kr)(Kr)(Kr)
Sweden's top five-star hotel enjoys a great location on the Norrmalm waterfront. This hotel also features two restaurants from Michelin-starred chef Mathias Dahlgren along with the Cadier Bar, renowned for its extraordinary cocktails.

Hotel Diplomat

MAP P3 ■ Strandvägen 7c ■ 08 459 68 00 ■ www.diplomathotel.com ■ (Kr)(Kr)(Kr)
A classical hotel in the heart of Östermalm, an exclusive district of Stockholm, it offers lovely views over the water to nearby Djurgården and Skeppsholmen, with vintage tramcars passing by along Strandvägen in the summer. The plush cocktail bar is a trendy spot to relax in at the end of a day's sightseeing.

Hotel Rival

MAP C5 ■ Mariatorget 3 ■ 08 545 789 00 ■ www.rival.se ■ (Kr)(Kr)(Kr)
The brainchild of ABBA legend Benny Andersson, Hotel Rival is one of the trendiest places to stay in Stockholm. Situated by a leafy square in the lively Södermalm district, the hotel hosts regular DJ events in its stylish bar. The excellent restaurant has a lovely outdoor terrace in the summer.

Lydmar Hotel

MAP D3 ■ Södra Blasieholmshamnen 2 ■ 08 22 31 60 ■ www.lydmar.com ■ (Kr)(Kr)(Kr)

A luxury hotel with a boutique feel, peacefully overlooking the harbour at Blasieholmen. With sea views there is a discreet second-floor terrace for sipping cocktails. Hotel guests have access to the nearby Grand Hotel's spa and fitness suite.

Nobis Hotel

MAP M2 ■ Norrmalmstorg 2–4 ■ 08 614 10 00 ■ www.nobishotel.se ■ (Kr)(Kr)(Kr)

At this contemporary luxury hotel the emphasis is on timeless chic and optimum function. Set in the heart of the city, it features an Italian-style restaurant and a more relaxed bistro, plus the Gold Bar and Lounge.

Boutique and Unique Hotels

The Winery Hotel

Rosenborgsgatan 20 ■ 08 14 60 00 ■ www.thewineryhotel.se ■ (Kr)

An industrial-chic wine-themed hotel on the fringes of Stockholm near the shores of Brunnsviken lake, this hotel is within easy reach of the centre. There is a restaurant, wine bar, on-site winery, gym, and rooftop terrace with an outdoor pool.

Berns Hotel

MAP M3 ■ Näckströmsgatan 8 ■ 08 566 32 00 ■ www.berns.se ■ (Kr)(Kr)

A boutique hotel, Berns is right in the city centre and an ideal choice for those interested in the city's nightlife. The hotel's own nightclub features world-famous and top local DJs.

Elite Hotel Marina Tower

Saltsjöqvarns kaj 25 ■ 08 555 702 00 ■ www.elite.se/sv/hotell/stockholm/hotel-marina-tower ■ (Kr)(Kr)

A waterfront hotel set in a former 19th-century mill on the Nacka shore, Marina Tower can be reached by commuter ferry from the city centre. The leisure facilities include a Turkish hammam as well as a swimming pool.

Haymarket by Scandic

MAP C3 ■ Hötorget 13–15 ■ 08 517 267 00 ■ www.scandichotels.com/haymarket ■ (Kr)(Kr)

Inhabiting the former premises of the famous old PUB department store, this indulgent Scandic signature hotel harks back to a 1920s era of optimism and elegance, with free room service, a lifestyle concierge and even in-room bartenders.

Hotel Kungsträdgården

MAP D5 ■ Västra Trädgårdsgatan 11B ■ 08 440 66 50 ■ www.hotelkungstradgarden.se ■ (Kr)(Kr)

Housed in a renovated 18th-century building in central Stockholm, Hotel Kungsträdgården is situated next to the King's garden and close to the shopping districts. The rooms are individually decorated in Gustavian style and offer an old-world charm.

Miss Clara by Nobis

MAP C2 ■ Sveavägen 48 ■ 08 440 67 00 ■ www.missclarahotel.com ■ (Kr)(Kr)

This sleek, urban hotel, situated in a former girls' school, is perfectly located for exploring central Stockholm. Expect rooms with cool, modern, black-and-white furnishings, wood parquet floors and designer linens and toiletries. There is a bar and restaurant, too.

Mornington Hotel

MAP N1 ■ Nybrogatan 53 ■ 08 507 330 00 ■ www.mornington.se ■ (Kr)(Kr)

This charming boutique hotel is located in the heart of Östermalm. A library with 4,000 books is one of the outstanding features of this hotel. It also has a patio garden in summer.

Story Hotel

MAP N2 ■ Riddargatan 6 ■ 08 545 039 40 ■ www.storyhotels.com ■ (Kr)(Kr)

A quirky boutique hotel, the Story is a lively place with a touch of class. It has a "retro" modern restaurant, and DJs play music in the bar four nights a week. The hotel offers a variety of room types to choose from.

Hotel Skeppsholmen

MAP Q5 ■ Gröna gången 1 ■ 08 407 23 50 ■ www.hotelskeppsholmen.com ■ (Kr)(Kr)(Kr)

This hotel has earned rave reviews as one of the hippest places to stay in the city. It combines the atmosphere of a building from the 17th-century with modern design and is on a beautiful city island with good bus connections to the centre.

Hotel with Urban Deli

MAP C2 ■ Sveavägen 44 ■ 08 30 30 50 ■ www.hotelwith.se ■ (Kr)(Kr)(Kr)

Having forged a strong reputation in the food business, Urban Deli have opened their first hotel, which is based entirely underground. None of the rooms have windows, but all of them have a state-of-the-art air purifying system, powerful sound and media systems and high-speed Wi-Fi access.

Villa Källhagen

MAP F3 ■ Djurgårdsbrunnsvägen 10 ■ 08 665 03 00 ■ www.kallhagen.se ■ (Kr)(Kr)(Kr)

Located by the canal in Djurgården, this refined hotel is a peaceful place to stay and is within easy reach of the city centre on public transport. The rooms are all tastefully decorated, and the premises also house a highly rated restaurant.

Mid-Range Hotels

Park Inn by Radisson Hammarby Sjöstad Hotel

Midskeppsgatan 6 ■ 08 505 070 00 ■ www.parkinn.com ■ (Kr)

This hotel offers modern conveniences in one of Stockholm's ecofriendly districts, Hammarby Sjöstad. Facilities include a sauna, a gym and a restaurant. Skip across the canal by boat, then take a bus to the city centre.

Scandic Anglais

MAP M1 ■ Humlegårdsgatan 23 ■ 08 517 340 00 ■ www.scandichotels.se ■ (Kr)

The buzz in this hotel is all about the music – with DJs playing six nights a week. There are 230 standard rooms with wooden flooring. Dine in its restaurant or pick up a drink from one of its popular bars. A buffet breakfast is included in the rate.

Scandic Continental

MAP C3 ■ Vasagatan 22 ■ 08 517 342 00 ■ www.scandichotels.com ■ (Kr)

Rebuilt to accommodate the construction of a railway tunnel under the site, the Scandic Continental is one of the group's most state-of-the-art hotels. Facilities include a gym, a car park, a good restaurant and several bars, including a lovely rooftop terrace in summer.

Scandic Malmen

MAP D5 ■ Götgatan 49–51 ■ 08 517 347 00 ■ www.scandichotels.com ■ (Kr)

An ideal base for exploring the buzzing heart of the vibrant Södermalm area, the Malmen overlooks large Medborgarplatsen, with SoFo just a couple of minutes' walk away. The hotel features a busy late-night bar-restaurant, while the adjoining Lilla Hotellbaren hosts live DJs and gigs, many of which are free to enter.

August Strindberg Hotell

MAP J1 ■ Tegnérgatan 38 ■ 08 32 50 06 ■ www.hotellstrindberg.se ■ (Kr)(Kr)

A lovely little garden where guests enjoy breakfast in summer is the highlight of the August Strindberg. The hotel is tucked away on a quiet side street just off the most interesting part of Drottninggatan and is close to all shops.

Central Hotel

MAP K2 ■ Vasagatan 38 ■ 08 566 208 00 ■ www.central.hotelistockholm.com ■ (Kr)(Kr)

In an excellent location almost opposite the main railway station and ideal for arrivals from all city airports, the comfortable Central Hotel is renowned for its friendly welcome. It is an affordable option in the heart of the city.

Clarion Hotel Stockholm

MAP D6 ■ Ringvägen 98 ■ 08 462 10 00 ■ www.nordicchoicehotels.com ■ (Kr)(Kr)

The hotel is located in a residential area of Södermalm and is close to the Skanstull Tunnelbana station as well as famous sights such as the Royal Palace and Globen. The cool upstairs bar is a popular meeting spot.

Elite Adlon

MAP K2 ■ Vasagatan 42 ■ 08 402 65 00 ■ www.adlon.se ■ (Kr)(Kr)

With an exterior that evokes the style of the 1950s, this hotel offers all modern facilities. In a busy location close to the city shops, it is also handy for the coach arrivals from the airports.

Elite Hotel Arcadia

MAP D1 ■ Körsbärsvägen 1 ■ 08 566 215 00 ■ www.elite.se ■ (Kr)(Kr)

Set in a quiet area, this hotel is close to Tekniska Högskolan Tunnelbana station which provides quick links to the centre. It is also a short stroll to the bars and restaurants of Vasastan. Apartments with kitchenettes cater for guests on longer stays.

Rex Hotel

MAP C2
■ Luntmakargatan 73 ■ 08 16 00 40 ■ www.rexhotel.se ■ (Kr)(Kr)
Housed in a simple, 19th-century townhouse this homely hotel features exposed brick walls and colourful furnishings. Located in the heart of the city, it is a block away from Sveavägen, and is also close to a range of restaurants and bars

Hotel At Six

MAP M3
■ Brunkebergstorg 6 ■ 08 578 828 00 ■ www.hotelatsix.com ■ (Kr)(Kr)(Kr)
Centrally located, At Six has over 300 luxurious rooms decorated with sleek, contemporary furnishings. The hotel's sophisticated restaurant and two stylish bars are popular with the city's residents as well guests. It is also home to the iconic Hosoi, a state-of-the-art music bar that hosts international DJs, record collectors, as well as intimate concerts.

Hotel Wellington

MAP E2 ■ Storgatan 6 ■ 08 667 09 10 ■ www.wellington.se ■ (Kr)(Kr)(Kr)
This laid-back and simple Östermalm hotel is well-suited for Skansen and Gröna Lund, along with the Strandvägen waterfront, the tram line and all city centre attractions and amenities. The rooms are very comfortable and individually styled with hardwood floors. Some rooms have balconies. The rate includes breakfast, and there is a sauna and a restaurant.

Budget Hotels

Hotel Anno 1647

MAP D5 ■ Mariagränd 3 ■ 08 442 16 80 ■ www.anno1647.se ■ (Kr)
Situated in two former townhouses from the 17th and 18th centuries, Anno 1647 is on a side street just off Götgatan, one of Södermalm's main shopping and drinking streets. The hotel is just a few steps away from the Slussen Tunnelbana and bus station, making for excellent transport links.

Hotel Attaché

Cedergrensvägen 16, Hägersten ■ 08 18 11 85 ■ www.aparthotel.se ■ (Kr)
A little out of town in a quiet residential area, Attaché has 60 rooms in varying sizes to choose from, and breakfast is included in the room prices. The hip Landet bar and restaurant is nearby if you want to go out in the neighbourhood.

Hotel Bema

MAP C2 ■ Upplandsgatan 13 ■ 08 23 26 75 ■ www.hotelbema.se ■ (Kr)
Facing the Tegnérlunden park and with an indoor courtyard garden, Bema has a pleasant location, right in the city. It is a good choice for anyone looking for a central hotel at a fair price.

Hotel Micro

MAP C2 ■ Tegnérlunden 8 ■ 08 545 455 69 ■ www.hotelmicro.se ■ (Kr)
The theme of this hotel is small rooms at small prices. The rooms are windowless and bathroom facilities shared, but if the aim is to explore the city and you want a central place to sleep, it offers a genuine budget price.

Hotel Tre Små Rum

MAP C5 ■ Högbergsgatan 81 ■ 08 641 23 71 ■ www.tresmarum.se ■ (Kr)
This is a superb-value option in a convenient location in Södermalm, close to the Tunnelbana and local train stations. The rooms are cosy and comfortable; breakfast is included in the price.

Motel L Hammarby Sjöstad

Hammarby allé 41 ■ 08 409 026 00 ■ ligula.se/motel-l ■ (Kr)
Modern design comes at a budget price at Motel L, where all rooms have Swedish Carpe Diem beds, rain showers and air conditioning. The communal area is a big, bright space where guests can rest, work or have a drink.

Quality Hotel Nacka

Värmdövägen 84, Nacka ■ 08 506 160 00 ■ www.choicehotels.se ■ (Kr)
Alongside a pool, sauna and a decent restaurant, this has 162 comfortable rooms. In summer, guests can enjoy a meal or drink on the beautiful terrace. There is free parking outside the entrance.

The Red Boat Hotel

MAP C4
■ Södermälarstrand Kajplats 10 ■ 08 644 43 85 ■ www.theredboat.com ■ (Kr)
A novel place to stay is on this boat moored close to the Old Town. There are two boats – a hotel and a hostel; the wooden-panelled cabins on the hotel boat are the cosiest option.

For a key to hotel price categories *see p112*

Connect Hotel City

MAP A2 ■ Alströmergatan 41 ■ 08 441 02 20 ■ www.connecthotel.se ■ (Kr)(Kr)
Quite basic in its approach, with some very small rooms, this hotel offers good rates for its location in the liveliest part of Kungsholmen. Try to make the most of the early booking discount.

Hotel Zinkensdamm

MAP B5 ■ Zinkens Väg 20 ■ 08 616 81 10 ■ www.zinkensdamm.com ■ (Kr)(Kr)
Situated in Tantolunden park on Södermalm, Hotel Zinkensdamm includes breakfast and internet access in its price; it has a bar and restaurant, too. It is both a hotel and hostel, and is a pleasant place to stay. There are bicycles available for hire.

Unique Hotel

MAP K1 ■ Kammakargatan 62 ■ 08 796 96 00 ■ www.uniquehotel.se ■ (Kr)(Kr)
Located very close to the bustling shopping street Drottninggatan, the Unique Hotel offers large rooms with high ceilings and mullioned windows. Choose between a room with a private bathroom or shared facilities.

B&Bs, Hostels and Apartments

Bed & Breakfast Stockholm at Mariatorget

MAP C5 ■ Torkel Knutssonsgatan 35 ■ 07 057 972 00 ■ (Kr)
Set in the same building as the entrance to the Mariatorget Tunnelbana station are these modern rooms. There are two one- or two-person rooms available, or both can be booked to accommodate three or four people as there is a connecting door.

City Backpackers Inn

MAP K2 ■ Upplandsgatan 2a ■ 08 20 69 20 ■ www.citybackpackers.org ■ (Kr)
This classic hostel has plenty of character, free internet, free pasta, laundry, a guest kitchen and very helpful staff. There is a variety of rooms from which to choose.

Globen Bed & Breakfast

Dammtrappgatan 13 ■ 07 367 980 60 ■ www.globenvilla.se ■ (Kr)
Live like a local in a typical Swedish wooden house with a pretty garden in a residen tial part of Stockholm near Globen and its underground station. There is a fully equipped cottage and also a studio.

Långholmen Hotel and Youth Hostel

MAP A5 ■ Långholmsmuren 20 ■ 08 720 85 00 ■ www.langholmen.com ■ (Kr)
Staying in a prison cell may not be everyone's dream – but that is the unique appeal of this former jail, which saw its last prisoners in 1975. It is now a fantastic modern hotel and hostel on the central island of Långholmen.

Rygerfjord Hotel and Hostel

MAP C4 ■ Söder Mälarstrand, Kajplats 12–14 ■ 08 84 08 30 ■ www.rygerfjord.se ■ (Kr)
A former Norwegian ferry boat, this has been converted into a hotel and hostel while retaining its nautical feel. Some rooms overlook Lake Mälaren with fine views across to the City Hall.

Stockholm Classic

MAP B5 ■ Lundagatan 31 ■ 07 086 12 24 ■ www.classicstockholm.com ■ (Kr)
On a pleasant street close to the Zinkensdamm Tunnelbana station, this has double rooms with views over Lake Mälaren and the city. It also has ship-cabin-style rooms. Guests can make use of the fully equipped kitchen.

Stockholm Hostel

MAP A2 ■ Alströmergatan 15 ■ 07 015 655 25 ■ www.stockholmhostel.se ■ (Kr)
This air-conditioned hostel is in Kungsholmen, a five-minute ride on the Tunnelbana from Stockholm Central station. Each room has a private bathroom. Guests can prepare meals in the two communal kitchens.

Biz Apartment Gärdet

Sehlstedtsgatan 67 ■ 08 578 553 00 ■ www.bizapartmenthotel.se/gardet ■ (Kr)(Kr)
This hotel has 175 classy apartments; you can choose between one- and two-bedroom apartments or a range of studios that are ideal for the solo traveller. There are some good deals for those wanting extended stays of a few weeks or months. Biz also has other hotels in different areas such as Solna and Hammarby Sjöstad.

Hostel af Chapman

MAP P5 ■ Flaggmansvägen 8 ■ 08 463 22 80 ■ www.svenskaturistforeningen.se ■ (Kr)(Kr)

Stay on a 19th-century ship or in the craftsmen house on Skeppsholmen, overlooking the Royal Palace and near many of the city's main museums. For the best value, take a bed in a shared cabin, though there are private rooms available, too.

Guldgränd Hotel Apartments

MAP D5 ■ Guldgränd 5 ■ 08 641 40 64 ■ www.secondhomeapartments.se/guldgrand ■ (Kr)(Kr)

In a 17th-century building not far from the Slussen Tunnelbana station in a busy part of Södermalm, Guldgränd has spacious and stylish single, double and triple rooms as well as family apartments.

Out-of-Town Accommodation

Good Morning+ Hagersten

Vastertorpsvägen 131 ■ 08 556 323 30 ■ www.ligula.se/goodmorninghotels/hagersten ■ (Kr)

Located on the southern approach to Stockholm, near the furniture retailer IKEA, this hotel offers high standards at reasonable prices. Its friendly, multilingual staff make it a popular choice.

Jumbo Stay

Jumbovägen 4, Arlanda Airport ■ 08 593 604 00 ■ www.jumbostay.com ■ (Kr)

Anyone who has ever wished to spend a night in their own private bedroom on an aeroplane, can have just that on this converted 747 airliner at Arlanda Airport.

Kastellet Bed & Breakfast

Vaxholms Kastell, Vaxholm ■ 08 541 330 35 ■ www.kastelletbnb.se ■ (Kr)

Set in the ancient fort of Vaxholm, this B&B is a good base for exploring the archipelago. Most ferries out of central Stockholm stop at this town, and from there it is easy to reach some of the islands by boat in a short time.

Clarion Hotel Gillet

Dragarbrunnsgatan 23, Uppsala ■ 01 868 18 00 ■ www.clarionhotelgillet.com ■ (Kr)(Kr)

The location in central Uppsala makes this hotel a good base to explore the city. Clarion Hotel Gillet has modern rooms and music nights in the bar.

Grand Hotel Saltsjöbaden

Hotellvägen 1, Saltsjöbaden ■ 08 506 170 00 ■ www.grandsaltsjobaden.se ■ (Kr)(Kr)

Inspired by Hôtel de Paris in Monte-Carlo, this is a majestic hotel. Sitting by an archipelago harbour, it is just 25 minutes by train to Slussen. The hotel often offers good-value deals.

Grinda Wärdshus

Södra bryggan, Grinda (archipelago) ■ 08 542 494 91 ■ www.grinda.se ■ (Kr)(Kr)

An old farmhouse set among fields and with an atmospheric summer harbour café-bar, this hotel allows guests to make the most of Grinda island's simple charm. Breakfast is included.

Hotel J

Ellensviksvägen 1, Nacka Strand ■ 08 601 30 00 ■ www.hotelj.com ■ (Kr)(Kr)

By the waterside in the inner archipelago with connections to the city by boat, Hotel J has a New England nautical theme (think wicker and blue and white). It is a great summer destination in which to unwind.

Yasuragi Hasseludden

Hamndalsvägen 6, Saltsjö-Boo ■ 08 747 64 00 ■ www.yasuragi.se ■ (Kr)(Kr)

This spa hotel offers both western and traditional Japanese rooms as well as a variety of rejuvenating treatments (including a complimentary dinner). There is also a tranquil Japanese-style garden leading down to the water.

Sigtuna Stads Hotell

Stora Nygatan 3, Sigtuna ■ 08 592 501 00 ■ www.sigtunastadshotell.se ■ (Kr)(Kr)(Kr)

This is Sweden's smallest five-star hotel. Dating from 1909, Sigtuna Stads has been very tastefully restored to retain its original elegance. During the summer guests can eat dinner overlooking the waters of Sigtunaviken.

Stallmästaregården Hotel

Norrtull ■ 08 610 13 00 ■ www.stallmastaregarden.se ■ (Kr)(Kr)(Kr)

A former coaching inn from the 1700s, this hotel, set close to Hagaparken, overlooks Brunnsviken lake. Although further afield, it is still a reasonable walk or a short bus ride to bars and restaurants around Odenplan.

***For a key to hotel price categories** see p112*

General Index

Page numbers in **bold** refer to main entries.

A

ABBA 6, 29
  ABBA The Museum 42, 78
Accommodation 111–17
Acne Studios 57
Adolf Frederik 25
Adolf Fredriks Kyrka 40, 66, 71
Af Chapman 87, 117
Air travel 106, 107
Akkurat 51, 96
Alcohol 47, 59, 108
Alunda Elk 33
Amusement parks *see* Gröna Lund
Ängsö Nationalpark 17
Apartments 111, 117
Arholma 17
ArkDes 58, 88
Arlanda Airport 106, 107, 115
Ascension Day 61
Asplund, Gunnar 71

B

B&Bs 111, 115, 117
Baltic Sea Science Center 13
Banking 110
Bars *see* Pubs and bars
Beaches 58
  Björnö 102
  Långholmen 93
  Saltsjöbaden 102
  Stockholm Archipelago 10, 16, 17, 18, 59
Bellman, Carl Michael 35
Bergianska Trädgården 45
Bergman, Ingmar 39
Bernadotte Apartments (Royal Palace) 26
Berns 51
Birger Jarl 38
Birka 100
Björnö 102
Björvik 18
Blå Gungan 89
Blasieholmen 87
  see also Gamla Stan, Skeppsholmen and Blasieholmen
Blue Hall (Stadshuset) 22
BluVelvet 89
Boat hiking 18
Boat trips
  Birka 100
  Drottningholm 25
  getting around by boat 107
  Mariefred 100
  Sigtuna 99
  Stockholm Archipelago 7, 16–19, 101
  winter 19
Bonniers Konsthall 58, 72
Book shops 89
Botanical Gardens (Uppsala) 101
Boutique hotels 113–14
Bredablick Tower (Skansen) 12
Bronze Age 32, 33
Budget hotels 116–17
Budget tips 59
Bünsowska House 78–9
Bus travel 106–7
Butterfly and Bird House (Hagaparken) 35

C

Café Opera 51
Café Tranan 50, 73, 74
Cafés 52–3
  Gamla Stan, Skeppsholmen and Blasieholmen 90
  Hagaparken 34
  Kungsholmen and Vasastan 74
  Norrmalm and City 68
  Östermalm and Djurgården 80
  Skansen 13
  Södermalm 96
Café & Bageri Pascal 96
Calexico's 54, 97
Camping, Stockholm Archipelago 19, 59
Car travel 106, 107
Carousels
  Gröna Lund 11, 28, 29, 59, 77
  Skansen 12
Castles and fortifications
  Gripsholm Castle (Mariefred) 100
  Kastellet 86
  Siaröfortet 16
  Steninge Slott 102
  Taxinga Slott 100, 102
Cathedrals
  Storkyrkan 36–7, 40, 86
  Uppsala 99, 101
  Västerås 102
Celsing, Johan 72
Celsing, Peter 65
Centralbadet 67
Ceramics 89
Charles XIV John 25
Children's attractions 48–9
Chinese Pagoda (Hagaparken) 35
Chinese Pavilion (Drottningholm) 25
Chokladkoppen 53, 87, 90
Christmas 61
Christmas Market 87
Churches 40–41
  Adolf Fredriks Kyrka 40, 66, 71
  Engelbrektskyrkan 41
  Gustav Vasa Kyrka 40
  Högalidskyrkan 40
  Katarina Kyrka 41, 95
  Maria Magdalena Kyrka 41, 95
  Riddarholmskyrkan 40, 85
  Royal Chapel 20–21, 26
  St Olof's (Sigtuna) 99
  St Paulskyrkan 94
  St Per's (Sigtuna) 99
  Sofia Kyrka 41, 45
  Tyska Kyrkan 40, 88
  see also Cathedrals
Clason, Isak Gustaf 79
Clothing shops 56–7, 89
Clubs 51, 58
Concerts, free 59

Copper Tents (Hagaparken) 34
Cottage rentals 18
Council Chamber (Stadshuset) 22
Court Theatre (Drottningholm) 24
COVID-19 111
Crafts 57, 89
Crayfish season 61
Crime 109
Currency 110
Customs information 108
Customs, local 111
Cycling 107
  bike hire 6, 59

D

Dalí, Salvador 43, 86
Danish rule 38
Day trips 98–103
De Chirico, Giorgio 86
Debaser 45, 51, 54, 58
Degas, Edgar 43
Dentists 108, 109
Department stores 56, 65, 67
Descartes, René 67
Design, Swedish 56–7, 89
Design House 56
Designtorget 56
Diplomatic quarter 79
Djurgården 6, 7, 45, 76, 79
  see also Östermalm and Djurgården
Djurgårdsbrunnsviken 77
Doctors 108
Dolls' houses (Nordiska Museet) 30
Drottningholm 7, 10, **24–5**, 43, 100
Drugs 108

E

Earth N More 89
Easter 61
Echo Temple (Hagaparken) 34
Economy 39
Edblad 89
Ekstedt 7, 55, 81
Eldh, Carl 22
Electrical appliances 110
Emergency services 108, 109
Engelbrektskyrkan 41
Ericcson Globe 47, 101
Ericsson, Lars Magnus 38
Erik XIV 27
Eriksson, Christian 22
Erlander, Tage 39
Eugen, Prince 23
Evert Taubes Terrass 88

F

Färgfabriken 47
Farm stays 18
Fasching 51
Ferries 106, 107
Festivals and events 60–61
  free 59
  Skansen 13
Fillipa K 57
Finnhamn 17
The Fishery Teatern 46
Fishing 19
Fjäderholmarna 6, 7, 16, 48
  places to eat 103
Fjällgatans Kaffestuga 46
The Flying Elk 7, 50, 91
Food and drink 55
  budget tips 59
  see also Cafés; Pubs and bars; Restaurants
Forsberg, Anders Gustaf 79
Forseth, Einar 22
Forum För Levande Historia 88
Fotografiska 42, 94
Foundation of Stockholm 38
Frank, Josef 56
Free attractions 58–9
Funicular Railway (Skansen) 12
Further Afield 98–103
  accommodation 115–16
  cafés and restaurants 103
  A Day Trip to Uppsala 101
  map 98–9
  sights 99–102

G

Galejan Fairground (Skansen) 12
Gällnö 17
Gamla Stan 6, 7, 38, 87
Gamla Stan, Skeppsholmen and Blasieholmen 84–91
  cafés, pubs and bars 90
  A Day in Gamla Stan, Skeppsholmen and Blasieholmen 87
  map 84–5
  places to eat 91
  shopping 89
  sights 85–8
Garbo, Greta 39, 46, 102
Gastrologik 7, 54, 81
Gauguin, Paul 43
Giant Dala Horse Statue 13
Glassware 13, 89
Globen 47, 101
Gold Room (Historiska Museet) 32
Golden Hall (Stadshuset) 22
Grand Hotel 87, 112
Grandpa 57
Granit 56
Greasy Spoon 7, 53, 96
Grinda 7, 17, 18
  places to stay 115
Gripsholm Castle (Mariefred) 100
Gröna Lund 6–7, 11, **28–9**, 49, 77
  season ticket 59
Guards' Tent (Drottningholm) 25
Gudrun Sjödén 89
Guest Apartments (Royal Palace) 26
Gustav II Adolf 14
Gustav III 25, 34, 85
  Gustav III's Museum of Antiquities (Royal Palace) 26
  Gustav III's Pavilion (Hagaparken) 35
  murder of 38
Gustav V 25
Gustav Vasa 30, 38, 101
Gustav Vasa Kyrka 40

H

Hagaparken 6, 11, **34–5**, 44, 99
Häktet 51, 96
Hall of State (Royal Palace) 26

Hammarbybacken 46
Hammarskjöld, Dag 39
Hamngatan 65, 67
Hazelius, Artur 30, 31
Health 108, 109
Hedvig Eleonora, Queen 24
Hermansson, Gustaf 41
Hilda Hilda 89
Historiska Museet 7, 11, **32–3**, 43, 77
History 38–9
Hjort, Roland 57
Hjorth, Bror, *Tek* 92
Hjortzberg, Olle 41
Högalidskyrkan 40
Homeware 56
Hornstulls Marknad 46
Hospitals 108
Hostels 111, 117
Hotels 111–17
Hötorget 67
Housing programme 39
Humlegården 45, 77

I

Ice skating 44, 48, 59, 66, 73
ID 109
Immigration 108
Industrialization 38
Ingmarsö 18
Insurance 108
International Workers' Day 61
Internet 110
Iris Hantverk 89
Itineraries 6–7
  A Day in Gamla Stan, Skeppsholmen and Blasieholmen 87
  A Day in Kungsholmen and Vasastan 73
  A Day in Norrmalm and City 67
  A Day in Östermalm and Djurgården 79
  A Day in Södermalm 95
  A Day Trip to Uppsala 101
  Four Days in Stockholm 6–7
  Two Days in Stockholm 6

J

Jewellery 89
Johan & Nyström 52, 96
Johansson, Jonny 57
Jones, Arne 45
Junibacken 48

K

Karl XI's Gallery (Royal Palace) 27
Karlson, Sven-Harry 71
Kastellet 86
Kastellholmen 86
Katarina Kyrka 41, 95
Katarinavägen 7
Kayaking 18
Knutsson, Fillipa 57
Krabat 89
Kristina, Queen 26, 67
Kulturhuset 65, 67
Kungliga Operan 65
Kungliga Slottet *see* Royal Palace
Kungsgatan 66, 67
Kungsholmen and Vasastan 6, 70–75
  cafés, pubs and bars 74
  A Day in Kungsholmen and Vasastan 73
  map 70
  places to eat 75
  sights 71–3
Kungstornen 66
Kungsträdgården 44, 66–7
Kvarnen 50–51, 96

L

Lake Mälaren 23, 38, 85, 86, 93
  boat trips 7, 25, 43, 99, 107
  skating 59
Landet 51, 103
Långholmen 46, 93
Language 111, 126–8
Larsson, Carl 43
Larsson, Stieg 94
Lennakatten Narrow Gauge Railway (Uppsala) 101, 102
LGBTQ+ safety 109
Lilla Ego 54, 75
Lilla Hotellbaren 51
  Lindgren, Astrid 39
Lindh, Anna 41
Linnaeus, Carl 39, 45, 76, 77
Linnaeus Garden (Uppsala) 101
Livrustkammaren (Royal Armoury) 7, 59, 88
Lovisa Ulrika, Queen 24, 25
Lucia 61
Lundquist, Evert 25

M

Made in Stockholm 89
Maria from Viklau 32
Maria Magdalena Kyrka 41, 95
Mariatorget 94
Mariefred 100
Marielund 101
Markets
  Christmas Market 87
  Hornstulls Marknad 46
  Hötorget 67
  loppis (flea markets) 59
Marklund, Bror 33
Mathias Dahlgren 54, 91
Matisse, Henri 43, 86
Meatballs for the People 55, 97
Medborgarplatsen 93
Medelhavsmuseet 66
Mellqvist Kaffebar 53, 94, 95, 96
Metro (Tunnelbana) 104–5, 106
  artworks 58
Midnattsloppet 60
Midsummer's Eve 61
Milles, Carl 30, 67, 100
Milles, Olga 100
Millesgården 100
Million Programme 39
Mobile phones 110
Moderna Museet 7, 42–3, 86, 87
Money 110
  budget tips 59
Monteliusvägen 93, 95
Morfar Ginko 50, 96
Mosebacke 94, 95
Mosebacke Torg 94
Mulle Meck Lekpark 49
Museums and galleries 42–3
  ABBA The Museum 42, 78
  ArkDes 58, 88
  Bonniers Konsthall 58, 72

Museums and galleries (cont.)
Färgfabriken 47
Fotografiska 42, 94
free entry 58
Gustav III's Museum of Antiquities (Royal Palace) 26
Haga Parkmuseum 35
Historiska Museet 7, 11, **32–3**, 43, 77
Kulturhuset 65, 67
Leksaksmuseet 49, 95
Livrustkammaren (Royal Armoury) 7, 59, 88
Medelhavsmuseet 66
Moderna Museet 7, 42–3, 86, 87
Nationalmuseum 43, 85, 87
Naturhitoriska Riksmuseet 49, 99
Nobelmuseet 86, 88
Nordiska Museet 6–7, 11, **30–31**, 42, 78
Östasiatiska Museet 88
Postmuseum 88
Prince's Gallery (Stadshuset) 10, 23
Skansen 10, **12–13**, 43, 49, 78
Spritmuseum 47
Strindbergsmuseet 72
Studio of Evert Lundquist (Drottningholm) 25
Sven-Harrys Konstmuseum 71
Tekniska Museet 48
The Viking Museum 88
Tom Tits Experiment (Södertälje) 102
Torekällberget Outdoor Museum (Södertälje) 102
Tower Museum (Stadshuset) 23
Tre Kroner Museum (Royal Palace) 26
Tunnelbana artworks 58
Vasamuseet 6–7, 10, **14–15**, 42, 78

N

Nacka Strand 115
Nämdö 18
National Day 61
National holidays 61
National Library of Sweden 45
National parks
Ängsö Nationalpark 17
Tyresta National Park 102
Nationalmuseum 43, 85, 87
Nature Path (Drottningholm) 24
Naturhitoriska Riksmuseet 49, 99
New Year's Eve 61
Nightlife 51, 58
Nilsson, Gustav 29
Nilsson, Magnus 46
Nobel, Alfred 39, 47
Nobel Banquet 23
Nobel Day 61
Nobel Prize 23, 27
Nobelmuseet 86, 88
Nordiska Museet 6–7, 11, **30–31**, 42, 78
Norr Mälarstrand 72, 73
Norrmalm and City 64–9
cafés, pubs and bars 68
A Day in Norrmalm and City 67
map 64
places to eat 69
sights 65–7
Norrmalmstorg 65
Norröra 16
Norrtull 116
Notke, Bernt 40
Nya Carnegiebryggeriet 50, 103
Nytorget Urban Deli 54, 95, 97

O

Odenplan 71, 73
Off the beaten track 46–7
Öja 17
Olof Palme's Plaque and Grave 66, 67
Olympic Games (1912) 38
Opening hours 110–11
Opera 65
Öresund toll bridge 106
Oscar I 25
Oscar II 25
Östasiatiska Museet 88
Östberg, Ragnar 22
Östermalm and Djurgården 76–81
cafés, pubs and bars 80
A Day in Östermalm and Djurgården 79
map 76
places to eat 81
sights 77–9
Östra Lagnö 17
Östra Södermalms steam railway 100
Oval Room (Stadshuset) 23

P

Palaces
Drottningholm 7, 10, **24–5**, 43, 100
Haga ruins 35
Royal Palace 6–7, 11, **26–7**, 43, 85, 87
Palme, Olof 39, 40
plaque and grave 66, 67
Pappa Ray Ray 50, 96
Parks and gardens 44–5
Bergianska Trädgården 45
Botanical Gardens (Uppsala) 101
Djurgården 6, 7, 45, 76, 79
Drottningholm 25, 58
Gröna Lund 6–7, 11, **28–9**, 49, 77
Hagaparken 6, 11, **34–5**, 44, 99
Humlegården 45, 77
Kungsträdgården 44, 66–7
Linnaeus Garden (Uppsala) 101
Millesgården 100
Rålambshovsparken 73
Rosendals Trädgård 45, 53, 77, 80
Skansen 6–7, 10, **12–13**, 43, 78
Skinnarviksparken 45

Parks and gardens (cont.)
Stadshuset Gardens 23
Stora Skuggan 44
Tantolunden 44, 95
Vasa Museum Garden 15
Vasaparken 44, 73
Vinterviken 47
Vitabergsparken 45
see also National parks
Passports 108, 109
Pedestrians 107
Persikan 94
Personal security 109
Petite France 6, 52–3, 73, 74
Phrase book 126–8
Picasso, Pablo 43, 86
Picnics 59
Popaganda 59, 61
Postal services 110
Postmuseum 88
Precht, Burchardt 40
Prince's Gallery (Stadshuset) 10, 23
Public holidays 61, 110–111
Pubs and bars 50–51
Gamla Stan, Skeppsholmen and Blasieholmen 90
Gröna Lund 29
Kungsholmen and Vasastan 74
Norrmalm and City 68
Östermalm and Djurgården 80
Södermalm 96
Punk Royale 55, 97

Q

Queen Hedvig Eleonora's State Bedroom (Drottningholm) 24
Queen Lovisa Ulrika's Library (Drottningholm) 24

R

Rail travel
arriving by train 106, 107
Lennakatten Narrow Gauge Railway 101
local trains 107
Östra Södermalms steam railway 100
Rålambshovsparken 73
Rehn, Jean Eric 24
Rembrandt 43
Restaurants 54–5
Gamla Stan, Skeppsholmen and Blasieholmen 91
Gröna Lund 29
Kungsholmen and Vasastan 75
Norrmalm and City 69
Östermalm and Djurgården 81
Skansen 13
Södermalm 97
Stadshuset 23
Stockholm Archipelago 18
Riche 50, 80
Riddarholmen 85
Riddarholmskyrkan 40, 85
Riksdag 58
Road travel 106
Rodebjer 56
Rödlöga 17
Rolfs Kök 54, 69
Roller coasters (Gröna Lund) 28, 77
Rörstrandsgatan 72
Rosendals Trädgård 45, 53, 77, 80
Rosendalsvägen 77
Royal Chapel 20–21, 26
Royal Guard 25, 27
Royal Palace 11, **26–7**, 43, 85
itineraries 6, 7, 87
Royal Armoury 7, 59, 88
Rubens, Peter Paul 43

S

Safety
government advice 108, 109
LGBTQ+ safety 109
personal security 109
St Paulskyrkan 94
Saltsjö-Boo 116
Saltsjöbaden 102
places to eat 103
places to stay 115
Sámi 30
Sandhamn 16
Saturnus 52, 80
Schultheis, Jacob 29
Sea travel 106, 107
Sergel, Johan Tobias 40
Sergels Torg 64, 65, 67
SF Bokhandeln 89
Shopping
Gamla Stan, Skeppsholmen and Blasieholmen 89
items to buy 57
Kungsholmen 72, 73
Östermalm 79
for Swedish design 56–7
SoFo 93
Siaröfortet 16
Sigtuna 99
places to eat 103
places to stay 115
Silverware 89
Själbottna 17
Skånegatan 94–5
Skansen 10, **12–13**, 43, 49, 78
itineraries 6, 7
Skansen Glassworks 13
Skeppsholmen
shoreline walk 87
see also Gamla Stan, Skeppsholmen and Blasieholmen
Skiing 46
Skinnarviksparken 45
Skogskyrkogården 102
Slussen 7, 86
Smoking 108
Snotty Sounds Bar 50, 94, 95, 96
Social Democrats 39
Södermalm 7, 82–3, 92–7
cafés, pubs and bars 96
A Day in Södermalm 95
map 92
places to eat 97
sights 93–5
Södertälje 102
Södra Teatern 94
Sofia Kyrka 41, 45
SoFo 93, 94–5
Solidaritet 51
Solna Centrum 58
Sosta 52, 68
Spas 46
Spritmuseum 47
Spy Bar 51
Stadsbiblioteket 71, 73

Stadshusbron 7
Stadshuset 7, 10, **22–3**, 71, 73
tower 6, 10, 23
Standard of living 39
State Apartments (Royal Palace) 27
Steamboats 19
Steninge Slott 102
Stock Exchange Building (Börshuset) 86
Stockholm Archipelago 8–9, 10, **16–19**, 101
itineraries 6, 7
things to do **18–19**
Stockholm Bauhaus Athletics 61
Stockholm Bloodbath 38, 86
Stockholm Culture Festival 60
Stockholm Fashion Week 60
Stockholm International Film Festival 61
Stockholm Marathon 60
Stockholm Pride 60, 95
"Stockholm Syndrome" 65
Stone Age 33
Stora Pelousen (Hagaparken) 34
Stora Skuggan 44
Storkyrkan 36–7, 40, 86
Stortorget 62–3, 86, 87
Story Tours 88
Strandvägen 79
Street food 46
Strindberg, August 11, 31, 39
Strindbergsmuseet 72
Studio of Evert Lundquist (Drottningholm) 25
Sturebadet 46
Sturecompagniet 51
Sturehof 55, 81
Sturekatten 52, 80
Stureplan 79
Stutterheim 89
Sveavägen 71
Sven-Harrys Konstmuseum 71
Svenskt Tenn 56–7
Sweden Solar System 47
Swedish Hasbeens 56, 95
Swedish Parliament 58
Swimming 46, 49, 58, 93, 95
Centralbadet 67
Stockholm Archipelago 18
Sturebadet 46

T

Tantolunden 44, 95
Taube, Evert 41
Taxes 111
Taxinga Slott 100, 102
Taxis 107
Tek (Hjorth) 92
Tekniska Museet 48
Telephones 110
Tessin, Nicodemus (the Younger) 26, 27
Thunberg, Greta 39
Tick-borne encephalitis 108
Time zone 110
Tom Tits Experiment (Södertälje) 102
Torekällberget Outdoor Museum (Södertälje) 102
Tourist information 111
Tower Museum (Stadshuset) 23
Trädgården 51
Travellers with specific requirements 110, 111
Trains *see* Rail travel
Trams 106–7
Travel
budget tips 59
getting to and around Stockholm 106–7
Tre Kroner Museum (Royal Palace) 26
Treasury (Royal Palace) 27, 85
Trouville 16
Turkish Pavilion (Hagaparken) 35
Tyresta National Park 102
Tyska Kyrkan 40, 88

U

Under Bron 51
Uppsala 98, 99
A Day Trip to Uppsala 101
places to eat 103
places to stay 115
Utö 17

V

Vasa (warship) 14–15, 78
Vasamuseet 6–7, 10, **14–15**, 42, 78
Vasaparken 44, 73
Vasastan *see* Kungsholmen and Vasastan
Västerås 102
Västerlångatan 87
Vaxholm 7, 17, 101
places to eat 103
places to stay 115
Vete-Katten 52, 67, 68
Vikings
Birka 100
Historiska Museet 33
The Viking Museum 88
Vinterviken 47
Visas 108, 109
Vitabergsparken 45

W

Walking
in Stockholm 107
tours 88
Walpurgis Night 61, 85
Water, drinking 108
Weather 110
Whyred 57
Wi-Fi 110
Wildlife
Baltic Sea Science Center 13
Butterfly and Bird House (Hagaparken) 35
city farm (Stora Skuggan) 44
Nature Path (Drottningholm) 24
Winter boat trips 19
Woman from Barum 33

Y

Youth hostels 117

Z

Zorn, Anders 43

Acknowledgments

This edition updated by

Contributor Taraneh Ghajar Jerven

Senior Editor Alison McGill

Senior Art Editor Stuti Tiwari

Project Editors Parnika Bagla, Rebecca Flynn

Editor Mark Silas

Picture Research Administrator Vagisha Pushp

Picture Research Manager Taiyaba Khatoon

Publishing Assistant Halima Mohammed

Jacket Designer Jordan Lambley

Senior Cartographer Subhashree Bharati

Cartography Manager Suresh Kumar

Senior DTP Designer Tanveer Zaidi

Senior Production Editor Jason Little

Senior Production Controller Samantha Cross

Deputy Managing Editor Beverly Smart

Managing Editors Shikha Kulkarni, Hollie Teague

Managing Art Editor Sarah Snelling

Senior Managing Art Editor Priyanka Thakur

Art Director Maxine Pedliham

Publishing Director Georgina Dee

DK would like to thank the following for their contribution to the previous editions: Paul Eade, Malcolm Jack

The publisher would like to thank the following for their kind permission to reproduce their photographs:
Key: a-above; b-below/bottom; c-centre; f-far; l-left; r-right; t-top

123RF.com: Jon Bilous 64cla; Boris Breytman 30bc; Hans Christiansson 66b; levgenii Fesenko 77tr; Stefan Holm 19cl; jorisvo 40cla; Mikhail Markovskiy 76tr; Olga Miltsova 100-1; svglass 39tr.

Alamy Stock Photo: Banana Pancake 4cr; Frank Chmura 55bl, 101cl; Mikael Damkier 82-3; Chad Ehlers 58tr, 93b; Peter Forsberg 53b; Bjorn Grotting 35crb; Alex Hammond 51tr; Dave G. Houser 31tl; imageBROKER / Matthias Graben 4clb; Johner Images 35bl, 61br; Interfoto 11clb; Henryk Kotowski 61cl; Art Kowalsky 78-9; Douglas Lander 103b; Franz Marc Frei 18tr; Hercules Milas 11tl; Prisma by Dukas Presseagentur GmbH / Chmura Frank 46tr; Maria Swärd 16-7; William Uzuriaga 60cb; Zoonar / Olaf Pokorny 11br.

© ArkDes: Nikolaj Alsterdal 88t.

AWL Images: Mauricio Abreu 12-3; David Bank 4cla; Nordic Photos 2tl, 4cl, 4b, 8-9.

Operaka ällarens Bakficka: 69br.

Bonniers Konsthall: 72cla.

Brewdog Kungsholmen: Mikael Goransson 74b.

Centralbadet, Stockholm: Magnus Torle 67cl.

Designtorget: Jean-Baptiste Beranger 56tr.

Dorling Kindersley: The Golden Hall, Stockholm Stadshuset by Einar Forseth © DACS 2017 22-3.

Dreamstime.com: Arsty 84tr; Ruzanna Arutyunyan 10cla; Roksana Bashyrova 85t; Per Björkdahl 17br, 99tr; Andrei Bortnikau 40bl; Boris Breytman 6cla, 25tl; Ryhor Bruyeu 41tr; Candy1812 10cl; Hans Christiansson 34clb; Marcin Ciesielski / Sylwia Cisek 23cr; Cumulus 72-3; Mikael Damkier 23tl, 47tl; Dimbar76 48t, 57tr; Eugenephoen 2tr, 36-7; Alexandre Fagundes De Fagundes 58-9; Joyfull 7cra; Kaleff 10cb, 11cra, 24-5, 42-3, 44b; Pavel Kavalenkau 28-9c; Sergii Koval 55tr; Andrey Kutsenko 23br; Alain Lacroix 4crb; Lerka555 77b; Mariagroth 59tr, 71b, 73tl; Mikhail Markovskiy 30-1, 86cl, 86br; Julie Mayfeng 49br; Moniphoto 100tr; Nadezhda 1906 59br; Nikonaft 87tl; Björkdahl Per 94-5tc; Pifu 70ca; Theresa Wing Yee Poon 6br; Rolf52 45tl, 60t; Tatiana Savvateeva 98ca; Tibisan 17cr; Alexander Tolstykh 22bl; Allan Wallberg 19tr; Nadezhda 1906 59br.

Earth N More: 89cl.

© Fotografiska, Jenny Hammar: 94cl.

Getty Images: Mauricio Abreu 78tl; Bettmann 39l; Michael Campanella 13tl; DEA / A. Dagli Orti 38ca; Elliot Elliot 19b; Werner Forman 100c; Johner Images 18bl; Ullstein Bild 38bl.

Grand Hôtel Stockholm: The Cadier Bar / Magnus Mårding 90b; Mathias Dahlgren / Magnus Mårding 54t.

Grandpa: 57cl.

Greasy Spoon: 53tr.

Grill: 75cra.

Gröna Lund: 28bl, 29bl, 49cl; Frans Hällquist 29cr.

Hornstulls Marknad: Patrik Linden Photography 46br.

Hotel Skeppsholmen: Restaurant La ånga Raden / Louise Billgert 91cra.

iStockphoto.com: cosmity 10b; Fotonen 102 cra; fotoVoyager 3tl, 4t, 62-3; master1305 11crb; mikdam 1; olaser 3tr, 104-5.

Junibacken: 48clb.

Kulturhuset: Matilda Rahm 65b.

Kungliga Operan: Markus Gårder 65tl.

Restaurang Kvarnen: Ivan da Silva 50-1, 96tr.

Moderna Museet: Åsa Lundén 43tl.

Nationalmuseum, Stockholn: 43cr.

Naturhistoriska riksmuseet: Martin Stenmark 99br.

Nordiska museet: 30clb, 31br.

Restaurant Pelikan: Christer Fahlström 97br.

Riche: Niklas Alexandersson 80cl.

The Royal Court (Kungliga Hovstaterna): 27tl; Alexis Daflos 20-1, 24br, 25br, 26cl, 26-7, 85br; Michael Steinberg 26bl; Gomer Swahn 35cra.

Skansen: Marie Andersson 13cr; Marie Ha åkansson 12bl.

Sofo: Justina Rosengren 92tl.

Spiritmuseum: Jonas Lindstro öm 47cr.

Statens Hstoriska Museum: 33tl; Magnus Aronson 33c; Gabriel Hildebrand 32br; Katarina Nimmervoll 32ca, 33crb.

SuperStock: age fotostock / Jörgen Larsson 45cr; Nordic Photos 16bl, 34-5, 50cra.

© SvenHarrys Konstmuseum: Per Myrehed 71tr.

Sveskt Tenn: 56b.

Tyresta National Park: Charl Mellin 102clb.

Världskulturmuseerna Stockholm: Ove Kaneberg 66tl.

Vasamuseet: Anneli Karlsson 14cl, 15br; Karolina Kristensson 15tl.

Vete-Katten: Susanna Bla åvarg 52 clb, 68t.

Cover

Front and spine: **iStockphoto.com:** mikdam

Back: **iStockphoto.com:** Angela Kotsell tr, mikdam b, petekarici crb, scanrail cla; **Picfair.com:** Simon Bath tl

Pull Out Map Cover

iStockphoto.com: mikdam

All other images © Dorling Kindersley

For further information see: www.dkimages.com

DK | Penguin Random House

First Edition 2013

Published in Great Britain by Dorling Kindersley Limited DK, One Embassy Gardens, 8 Viaduct Gardens, London SW11 7BW, UK

The authorised representative in the EEA is Dorling Kindersley Verlag GmbH. Arnulfstr. 124, 80636 Munich, Germany

Published in the United States by DK Publishing, 1745 Broadway, 20th Floor, New York, NY 10019, USA

Copyright © 2013, 2023 Dorling Kindersley Limited

A Penguin Random House Company

23 24 25 10 9 8 7 6 5 4

No part of this publication may be reproduced, stored in or introduced into a retrieval system, or transmitted in any form, or by any means (electronic, mechanical, photocopying, recording or otherwise) without the prior written permission of the copyright owner.

The publishers cannot accept responsibility for any consequences arising from the use of this book, nor for any material on third party websites, and cannot guarantee that any website address in this book will be a suitable source of travel information.

A CIP catalogue record is available from the British Library.

A catalogue record for this book is available from the Library of Congress.

ISSN 1479-344X

ISBN 978-0-2416-1297-2

Printed in Malaysia

www.dk.com

As a guide to abbreviations in visitor information blocks: ***Adm*** *= admission charge;* ***L*** *= Lunch;* ***D*** *= dinner.*

FSC www.fsc.org MIX Paper | Supporting responsible forestry FSC™ C018179

This book was made with Forest Stewardship Council™ certified paper – one small step in DK's commitment to a sustainable future.

For more information go to www.dk.com/our-green-pledge

Phrase Book

When reading the imitated pronunciation, stress the part which is underlined. Pronounce each syllable as if it formed part of an English word, and you will be understood sufficiently well. Remember the points below, and your pronunciation will be even closer to the correct Swedish.

Guidelines for Pronunciation

ai = as in 'fair' or 'stair'
ea = as in 'ear' or 'hear'
ew = like the sound in 'dew'
EW = try to say 'ee' with your lips rounded
oo = as in 'book' or 'soot'
OO = as in 'spoon' or 'groom'
r = should be strongly pronounced

Swedish Alphabetical Order

In the list below we have followed the Swedish alphabetical order. The following letters are listed after ***z***: ***å, ä, ö***.

In an Emergency

Help!	**Hjälp!**	*yelp*
Stop!	**Stanna!**	*stanna!*
Call a doctor!	**Ring efter en doktor!**	*ring efter ehn doktor*
Call an ambulance!	**Ring efter en ambulans!**	*ring efter ehn ambewlanss*
Call the police!	**Ring polisen!**	*ring poleesen*
Call the fire brigade!	**Ring efter brandkåren!**	*ring efter brandkawren*
Where is the nearest telephone?	**Var finns närmaste telefon?**	*vahr finnss nairmasteh telefawn*
Where is the nearest hospital?	**Var finns närmaste sjukhus?**	*vahr finnss nairmasteh shewkhews*

Communication Essentials

Yes	**Ja**	*yah*
No	**Nej**	*nay*
Please (offering)	**Varsågod**	*vahrshawgOOd*
Thank you	**Tack**	*tack*
Excuse me	**Ursäkta**	*ewrshekta*
Hello	**Hej**	*hay*
Goodbye	**Hej då/adjö**	*haydaw/ahyur*
Good night	**God natt**	*goonutt*
Morning	**Morgon**	*morron*
Afternoon	**Eftermiddag**	*eftermiddahg*
Evening	**Kväll**	*kvell*
Yesterday	**Igår**	*ee gawr*
Today	**Idag**	*ee dahg*
Tomorrow	**I morgon**	*ee morron*
Here	**Här**	*hair*
There	**Där**	*dair*
What?	**Vad?**	*vah*
When?	**När?**	*nair*
Why?	**Varför?**	*vahrfurr*
Where?	**Var?**	*vahr*

Useful Phrases

How are you?	**Hur mår du?**	*hewr mawr dew*
Very well, thank you.	**Mycket bra, tack.**	*mewkeh brah, tack*
Pleased to meet you.	**Trevligt att träffas.**	*trealvlit att traiffas*
See you soon.	**Vi ses snart.**	*vee seas snahrt*
That's fine.	**Det går bra.**	*dea gawr brah*
Where is/are …?	**Var finns …?**	*vahr finnss…*
How far is it to …?	**Hur långt är det till**	*hewr lawngt ea dea till*
Which way to …?	**Hur kommer jag till …?**	*hewr kommer yah till…*
Do you speak English?	**Talar du/ni engelska?**	*tahlar dew/nee engelska*
I don't understand	**Jag förstår. inte**	*yah furshtawr inteh*
Could you speak more slowly, please?	**Kan du/ni tala långsammare, tack?**	*kan dew/nee tahla lawngssamareh tack*
I'm sorry.	**Förlåt.**	*furrlawt*

Useful Words

big	**stor**	*stOOr*
small	**liten**	*leeten*
hot	**varm**	*varrm*
cold	**kall**	*kall*
good	**bra**	*brah*
bad	**dålig**	*dawleeg*
enough	**tillräcklig**	*tillraikleeg*
open	**öppen**	*urpen*
closed	**stängd**	*staingd*
left	**vänster**	*vainster*
right	**höger**	*hurger*
straight on	**rakt fram**	*rahkt fram*
near	**nära**	*naira*
far	**långt**	*lawngt*
up/over	**upp/över**	*ewp/urver*
down/under	**ner/under**	*near/ewnder*
early	**tidig**	*teedee*
late	**sen**	*sehn*
entrance	**ingång**	*ingawng*
exit	**utgång**	*ewtgawng*
toilet	**toalett**	*too-alett*
more	**mer**	*mehr*
less	**mindre**	*meendre*

Shopping

How much - is this?	**Hur mycket - kostar den här?**	*hewr mewkeh kostar dehn hair*
I would like …	**Jag skulle vilja…**	*yah skewleh vilya*
Do you have?	**Har du/ni …?**	*hahr dew/nee…*
I'm just looking	**Jag ser mig bara omkring**	*yah sear may bahra omkring*
Do you take credit cards?	**Tar du/ni kreditkort?**	*tahr dew/nee kredeetkoort*
What time do you open?	**När öppnar ni?**	*nair urpnar nee*
What time do you close?	**När stänger ni?**	*nair stainger nee*
expensive	**dyr**	*dewr*
cheap	**billig**	*billig*
size (clothes)	**storlek**	*stOOrlek*
white	**vit**	*veet*
black	**svart**	*svart*
red	**röd**	*rurd*
yellow	**gul**	*gewl*
green	**grön**	*grurn*
blue	**blå**	*blaw*
antique shop	**antikaffär**	*anteek-affair*
bakery	**bageri**	*bahgeree*
bank	**bank**	*bank*
book shop	**bokhandel**	*bOOkhandel*
cake shop	**konditori**	*konditoree*
chemist	**apotek**	*apoteak*
market	**marknad**	*marrknad*
newsagent	**tidningskiosk**	*teednings-cheeosk*
post office	**postkontor**	*posstkontOOr*
supermarket	**snabbköp**	*snabbchurp*
tobacconist's	**tobakshandel**	*tOObaks-handel*
travel agency	**resebyrå**	*reasseh-bewraw*

Sightseeing

art gallery	**konstgalleri**	*konnst-galleree*
church	**kyrka**	*chewrka*
garden	**trädgård**	*traidgawrd*
house	**hus**	*hews*

library	**bibliotek**	*beebleeotek*
museum	**museum**	*mewseum*
square	**torg**	*tohrj*
street	**gata**	*gahta*
tourist information office	**turist-informations-kontor**	*tureest-informashOOns kontOOr*
town hall	**stadshus**	*statshews*
closed for holiday	**stängt för semester**	*staingt furr semester*
bus station	**busstation**	*bewss-stashOOn*
railway station	**järnvägsstation**	*yairnvaigsstashOOn*

Staying in a Hotel

Do you have any vacancies?	**Har ni några lediga rum?**	*hahr nee nawgra lediga rewm*
double room with double bed	**dubbelrum med dubbelsäng**	*doobelrewm med doobel seng*
twin room	**dubbelrum med två sängar**	*doobelrewm med tvaw sengar*
single room	**enkelrum**	*enkelrewm*
room with a bath	**rum med bad**	*rewm med bahd*
shower	**dusch**	*dewsh*
key	**nyckel**	*newckel*
I have a reservation	**Jag har beställt rum**	*yah hahr bestellt rewm*

Eating Out

Have you got a table for…	**Har ni ett bord för…?**	*hahr nee ett bOOrd furr…*
I would like to reserve a table.	**Jag skulle vilja boka ett bord.**	*yah skewleh vilya bOOka ett bOOrd*
The bill, please.	**Notan, tack.**	*nOOtan, tack*
I am a vegetarian	**Jag är vegetarian**	*yah air vegetariahn*
waitress	**servitris**	*sairvitreess*
waiter	**servitör**	*sairviturr*
menu	**meny/matsedel**	*menew/mahtseadel*
fixed-price menu	**meny med fast pris**	*menew med fast prees*
wine list	**vinlista**	*veenlista*
glass of water	**ett glas vatten**	*ett glahss vatten*
glass of wine	**ett glas vin**	*ett glahss veen*
bottle	**flaska**	*flaska*
knife	**kniv**	*k-neev*
fork	**gaffel**	*gaffel*
spoon	**sked**	*shead*
breakfast	**frukost**	*frewkost*
lunch	**lunch**	*lewnch*
dinner	**middag**	*middahg*
main course	**huvudrätt**	*hewvewdrett*
starter	**förrätt**	*furrett*
dish of the day	**dagens rätt**	*dahgens rett*
coffee	**kaffe**	*kaffeh*

Menu Decoder

apelsin	*appelseen*	orange
bakelse	*bahkelse*	cake, pastry, tart
banan	*banahn*	banana
biff	*biff*	beef
bröd	*brurd*	bread
bullar	*bewllar*	buns
choklad	*shooklahd*	chocolate
citron	*sitrOOn*	lemon
dessert	*dessair*	dessert
fisk	*fisk*	fish
fläsk	*flaisk*	pork
forell	*fooraill*	trout
frukt	*fruckt*	fruit
glass	*glass*	ice cream
hummer	*hummer*	lobster
kallskuret	*kall-skuret*	cold meat
korv	*kohrv*	sausages
kyckling	*chewkling*	chicken
kött	*churtt*	meat
lamm	*lamm*	lamb
lök	*lurk*	onion
mineralvatten	*minerahl-vatten*	mineral water
mjölk	*m-yurlk*	milk
nötkött	*nurtchurtt*	beef
ost	*oost*	cheese
olja	*olya*	oil
potatis	*potahtis*	potatoes
ris	*rees*	rice
rostat bröd	*rostat brurd*	toast
räkor	*raikoor*	prawns
rött vin	*rurtt veen*	red wine
saft	*safft*	cordial
sill	*seell*	herring
skaldjur	*skahl-yewr*	seafood
smör	*smurr*	butter
stekt	*stehkt*	fried
salt	*sallt*	salt
socker	*socker*	sugar
soppa	*soppa*	soup
sås	*saws*	sauce
te	*tea*	tea
torr	*torr*	dry
ungsstekt	*ewngs-stehkt*	baked, roast
vispgrädde	*veesp-graiddeh*	whipped cream
vitlök	*veet-lurk*	garlic
vitt vin	*veett veen*	white wine
ägg	*aigg*	egg
äpple	*aippleh*	apple
öl	*url*	beer

Numbers

0	**noll**	*noll*
1	**ett**	*ett*
2	**två**	*tvaw*
3	**tre**	*trea*
4	**fyra**	*fewra*
5	**fem**	*fem*
6	**sex**	*sex*
7	**sju**	*shew*
8	**åtta**	*otta*
9	**nio**	*nee-oo*
10	**tio**	*tee-oo*
100	**(ett) hundra**	*(ett) hewndra*
200	**tvåhundra**	*tvawhewndra*
300	**trehundra**	*treahewndra*
400	**fyrahundra**	*fewrahewndra*
500	**femhundra**	*femhewndra*
1 000	**(ett) tusen**	*(ett) tewssen*

Time

one minute	**en minut**	*ehn meenewt*
one hour	**en timme**	*ehn timmeh*
half an hour	**en halvtimme**	*ehn halvtimmeh*
ten past one	**tio över ett**	*teeoo urver ett*
quarter past one	**kvart över ett**	*kvahrt urver ett*
half past one	**halv två**	*halv tvaw*
two o'clock	**klockan två**	*klockan tvaw*
13.00	**klockan tretton**	*klockan tretton*
16.30	**sexton och trettio**	*sexton ock trettio*
noon	**klockan tolv**	*klockan tolv*
midnight	**midnatt**	*meednatt*
Monday	**måndag**	*mawndahg*
Tuesday	**tisdag**	*teesdahg*
Wednesday	**onsdag**	*oonssdahg*
Thursday	**torsdag**	*toorsdahg*
Friday	**fredag**	*freadahg*
Saturday	**lördag**	*lurrdahg*
Sunday	**söndag**	*surndahg*

Selected Street Index

Allmänna Gränd R5
Amiralsvägen P5
Apelbergsgatan L2
Artillerigatan N3
Atlasmuren B2
Åsögatan D5
Banérgatan Q3
Barnhusgatan K2
Bergsgatan B3
Biblioteksgatan M2
Birger Jarlsgatan D3
Blasieholmsgatan N3
Blekholmsterrassen J3
Borgmästargatan E5
Brahegatan N1
Breda Gatan R6
Brunnsgatan M1
Brunnsgränd N5
Bryggargatan L2
Cardellgatan N1
Dalagatan J1
David Bagares Gata M1
Djurgårdsvägen R4
Drakenbergsgatan B5
Drottninggatan L2
Döbelnsgatan L1
Engelbrektsgatan D2
Eriksbergsgatan D2
Falkenbergsgatan R5
Floragatan D2
Folkungagatan E5
Fredsgatan L4
Gamla Brogatan K2
Grev Magnigatan P3
Grevgatan Q1
Gröna Gången P5
Grubbens Gata B3
Guldgränd M6
Gyllenstiernsgatan R2
Gås Gränd M5
Gästrikegatan B2
Götgatan D6
Hamngatan M3
Hantverkargatan J4
Heleneborgsgatan B5
Herkulesgatan L3
Holländargatan K1
Hovslagargatan N4
Humlegårdsgatan M1
Högalidsgatan B5
Högbergsgatan D5
Inedalsgatan B3
Jakobsbergsgatan M2
Jakobsgatan L4
Johannesgatan L1
Jungfrugatan P1
Järntorget M6
Kammakargatan K1
Kapellgränd D5
Kaplansbacken J4
Kaptensgatan P3
Karduansmakargatan L4
Karlavägen R2
Katarinavägen D5
Kindstugatan M5
Klara Norra Kyrkogata K2
Klarabergsgatan L3
Klarabergsviadukten K3
Klarastrandsleden K4
Kocksgatan D5
Kommendörsgatan N1
Kristinehovsgatan B5
Kungsholmsgatan B3
Kungsträdgårdsgatan M3
Kåkbrinken M5
Köpmangatan M5
Lilla Nygatan M5
Linnégatan R2
Ljusterögatan E6
Lundagatan B5
Luntmakargatan L1
Långa Gatan R5
Långa Raden P5
Lästmakargatan M2
Lützengatan Q1
Majorsgatan N1
Malmgårdsvägen E6
Malmskillnadsgatan L2
Malmtorgsgatan L3
Metargatan E6
Monteliusvägen L6
Munkbrogatan M5
Museikajen N4
Myntgatan M5
Målargatan L2
Mårten Trotzigs Gränd M6
Mäster Samuelsgatan L3
Narvavägen Q2
Nordenskiöldgatan R6
Norra Agnegatan B3
Norra Brobänken P4
Norra Stationsgatan A1
Norrlandsgatan M2
Nybergsgatan P1
Nybrogatan N2
Nybrokajen N3
Nytorgsgatan E5
Näckströmsgatan M3
Odengatan B2
Olof Palmes Gata K2
Olofsgatan L1
Oxenstiernsgatan F3
Oxtorgsgatan L2
Österlånggatan N5
Östermalmsgatan D2
Östgötagatan D5
Parmmätargatan J4
Pilgatan B3
Ploggatan E6
Prästgatan M5
Pryssgränd L6
Regeringsgatan M2
Renstiernas Gata E5
Repslagargatan D5
Riddargatan P2
Rigagatan R1
Ringvägen C6
Rosendalsvägen R4
Runebergsgatan D2
Rådmansgatan J1
Sankt Eriksgatan B2
Scheelegatan B3
Schönfeldts Gränd M5
Sergelgatan L2
Sibyllegatan N2
Sigtunagatan B2
Själagårdsgatan M5
Skeppargatan P3
Skeppsbron N5
Slöjdgatan L2
Slottsbacken M5
Slottskajen M4
Slussplan M6
Snickarbacken M1
Sofiagatan E6
Stadsgårdshamnen D5
Stadsgårdsleden D5
Stallgatan N3
Stora Nygatan M5
Storgatan R3
Storkyrkobrinken M5
Strandvägen R3
Strömgatan L4
Sturegatan N1
Styrmansgatan P2
Svartensgatan D5
Svartmangatan M5
Sveavägen L1
Svensksundsvägen P5
Söder Mälarstrand L6
Södra Blasieholmshamnen N4
Södra Brobänken P5
Tegnérgatan K1
Tengdahlsgatan E6
Terminalslingan K3
Tjärhovsgatan D5
Torsgatan J2
Torstenssonsgatan Q3
Trädgårdsgatan M3
Tunnelgatan L1
Tyska Brinken M5
Tysta Gatan Q1
Ulrikagatan R2
Upplandsgatan K1
Varvsgatan B5
Vasagatan K2
Vattugatan L3
Vegagatan B2
Villagatan D2
Väpnargatan N3
Värtavägen Q1
Västerlånggatan M5
Västra Brobänken P5
Yxsmedsgränd M5
Zinkens Väg B5